THE
POWER OF
AFRICENTRIC
CELEBRATIONS

THE POWER OF AFRICENTRIC CELEBRATIONS

Inspirations from the Zairean Liturgy

Nwaka Chris Egbulem

A Crossroad Herder Book
The Crossroad Publishing Company
New York

1996

The Crossroad Publishing Company
370 Lexington Avenue, New York, NY 10017

Printed in the United States of America

Library of Congress Cataloging-in-Publication Data

Egbulem, Nwaka Chris.
    The power of Africentric celebrations: inspirations from the
Zairean liturgy / Nwaka Chris Egbulem.
      p. cm.
    Includes bibliographical references and index.
    ISBN: 0-8245-1489-0
    1. Catholic Church–Zaire–Liturgy. 2. Catholic Church–Zaire–
Customs and practices. 3. Zaire–Church history–20th century.
I. Title.
BX1971.Z28E42   1996
264'.02096751–dc20   95-45165
                                            CTP

To the memory of my father,
Udealaukwu Alfred Egbulem,
priest, prophet, ancestor

Contents

7

Acknowledgments

Many people have played inspiring roles for me in the research and publication of this book. I thank the good Lord for the many thousands of people whom I have celebrated with in the two and half decades of my pastoral ministry on three continents. My family has been there every step of the way. A special appreciation to the church in Zaire for daring to dream and to pursue a project of African Christianity. Here in North America, the African American Catholic family joined me to dance the music and the rhythm.

My gratitude goes to David N. Power, O.M.I., who guided my academic journey at the Catholic University of America. I also thank the editors of *Missionhurst* magazine, who continue to chronicle the joys and pains of African Christianity.

Mrs. Shirley Brubaker of Michigan cheered me through seminary formation and beyond. I also thank God for Alex and Dory Szeles and their families in Pennsylvania for the strength and hope they continue to bring to our ministry.

Thanks to the directors, volunteers, and members of the Amen Foundation in Washington, D.C., who daily share and uphold our vision and mission worldwide. And to the entire membership of our Dominican Province of Nigeria, grace to you for the strength we share.

Introduction

For peoples of African descent, the entire life cycle presents itself as a continuous experience of celebration. From the period of life-before-conception through to life-after-life, African peoples live in a chain of rituals and events that mark the rhythm of existence. Events generate celebrations, and these in turn give meaning to living. Celebrations are the soul and spice of life. Of course, the nature of these celebrations differs from place to place, as do the content and style of the celebrations and the reasons for them.

There are, for example, marked differences between the ceremonies for naming a child, the ceremonies for the marriage of a young couple, and the ceremonies associated with new harvests. A funeral celebration for an elder of the village differs significantly from that of a very young person in the same village. The differences between one locality and another or between one African country and another can be very significant. Puberty rites among the Masai in Kenya (East Africa) have a unique spiritual, cultural, and sociological depth compared to such rites in West Africa. In all the celebrations, however, certain features remain constant. The people gather, women and men, young and old, the wealthy and the dependents; all come to share in the joys, hopes, and pains of life. In the celebrations there is extensive use of symbolism and

11

a powerful use of words and idioms. In story, testimonies, song, music, dance, acclamations, gestures, incantations, and libations, the people celebrate.

Wherever Africans have migrated either by choice or by chance, they have carried with them that hot blood of powerful celebration. In my travels on three continents, I have spent time listening, speaking, and sharing with many of our people. The testimony is strong and sound. No one else seems to match the joy we dance at childbirth, the pain we endure at funerals, the hope we celebrate at burials, or the peace we encounter in our memorials of our ancestors. The difficulties and tragedies of life are not able to exterminate the God-given drive in our people. Nor have hunger, drought, economic disasters on the African continent, or the devastating and humiliating experiences of slavery been able to erase that up-beat spirit of celebration. As an African proverb says, "The rain may beat on the leopard's skin for as long as it wants, but the Creator's designs are not washed off."

In the middle-belt region of Africa, that is, the region covered by West, Central, and East Africa, a trend was born in the middle of the twentieth century marked by growing respect for the ways peoples of African descent around the world live, worship, and celebrate. Protestant Christianity first caught the fire of that movement. In the meantime, the emergent Traditional African Christian Churches, many of which were founded by former converts to Protestantism, began to evolve forms of worship and celebration that gave resounding accent to the African heartbeat. A number of these churches were founded and pastored by women identified as "prophetesses," who put great emotion and life into their celebrations. The rest of the world began to take note. From then on, other Christian churches began to respect not only the gongs and drums of African life but also and especially the spiritual juice of Africa that give birth to the energetic celebrations.

How the Catholic faith is finally opening itself up to the riches of traditional African life and to the power of Africentric celebrations is the special interest of this book. The concept of "liturgical adaptation" clearly proposed at the Second Vatican Council was the starting point for the turnaround in the church's attitude toward African liturgical traditions. That concept soon yielded to the more dynamic concept called "liturgical inculturation," born in and sustained by a deep appreciation for the model and dynamism of the ultimate action of the incarnation of Jesus the Christ.

In 1984 an important ecclesiastical gathering was held in Kinshasa, Zaire. Over 70 bishops, archbishops, and cardinals, representing the 350 bishops in the episcopal conferences of Africa and Madagascar, were the formal participants. Informal participants were invited observers from around the world, including representatives of other Christian traditions, delegates of the Major Superiors of Religious Women and Men, and representatives of the laity. The episcopal conferences of Europe, Latin America, Asia, Canada, and the United States were also represented. The assembly had a worldwide representation of church hierarchy and theologians.

The participants had the occasion to join in the celebration of the Zairean liturgy at which a large number of the local people were present. Writing for American readers, Edward Braxton, an African American priest-participant who is now a bishop in Chicago, recounts:

> The uncluttered sanctuary was brightly painted in white, red, green, and black traditional African patterns. The flowing robes of the choir, ministers, and celebrants were woven in green, brown, and orange. The language was not the French of the colonialist but the native African tongue. The Rite began with the "announcer" dramatically coming down the aisle striking a gong-like

instrument, calling the assembly to prayer. The ministers
of the Mass entered in a swaying dance-like procession.
The solemn processional candles were alternated with
spear-like ornaments. The celebrant wore a very ample
and festive chasuble. His head was covered with a ceremonial cap that indicated that he represented the whole
clan, the people of God. He venerated the altar on all
four sides with great reverence. During the eucharistic
prayer, the sanctuary was surrounded by a circle of ministers moving in eloquent gestures of prayerful awe. The
Rite lasted about two hours, but it seemed much shorter
because of the rich atmosphere of prayer and celebration. The ebullience of the congregation was contagious.
Chants, applause, acclamation, spontaneous prayer, and
dialogue with the priest added to the familiar atmosphere. The music was extraordinary. Drums, tom-tom,
guitars, accordions, and ancient African instruments provided the background for the enthusiastic singing. And
everyone sang, the old, the young, men and women. The
church was packed and every participant was caught up
in the spiritual rapture of sound. As we sang, we sculpted
the air with our hands in clap-like gestures that embod-
ied the meaning of each song. Though we did not know
one word of the language, we never felt outside the bonds
of spiritual communion electrifying the congregation of
St. Alphonse de Kin-Matete. I do not believe that there is
anything like it anywhere else in the world. The Americans present agreed that praying in this way was an
experience of a lifetime.[1]

Calling the celebration of this Rite Zairois "a high point
of the symposium," Braxton concluded that "the Zairean Rite
Mass is perhaps the most creative response to Vatican II's
mandate for indigenous liturgical expression in the world."

Brian Hearne calls the Zairean Mass a "courageous new departure" paving the way for a possible African rite in the near future.[2]

In a remarkable way the church in Zaire, Central Africa, is playing a leadership role in this cause. In this book I will use as a point of reference the celebration of the Eucharist in Zaire popularly known as "Rite Zairois" (French for "Zairean rite"). The terms "Zairean rite," "Rite Zairois," "Zairean Mass," and "Zairean liturgy" will be used interchangeably to refer to the form of celebration of the Eucharist approved by the Vatican in 1988 for the Catholic dioceses of Zaire. I use the term "Africentric" to refer to forms of celebration that bear the dynamic marks of authentic Africanness, celebrations that radiate the genius and blessings of peoples of African descent. When I refer to characteristics of "Africans" and "African people," I am, of course, making broad generalizations that will have many exceptions. In my critique of the text and celebration of this liturgy, I will explore how that celebration has expressed aspects of authentic African worship and will try to discern both its graces and its weaknesses.

Peoples of African descent in North and South America have also been on a liturgical journey toward authenticity and affirmed personhood. African American bishops in the United States, the National Black Catholic Clergy Caucus (U.S.A.), and the National Black Catholic Congress (U.S.A.), for example, have all made clear statements regarding the need for in-depth reflection and action in the development of authentic and spirited worship in the communities. In this book I hope to help carve a path toward that healing goal. Our reflection also hopes to offer clues and challenges to liturgists, pastors, and ministers of other Christian communities and different cultural backgrounds, thus helping to create a broader awareness in the search for authentic worship among those congregations.

Chapter 1

Catholic Missionaries and African Rituals

When Catholic missionaries arrived in Africa with a theology already baked, parceled, and frozen to be delivered to our people, evangelization served as a mysterious, foreign tool mostly concerned with the invisible souls of men (and, occasionally, women). The missionaries' beliefs were clear and unequivocal. They believed that their arrival in a village marked the beginning of a new testament. Life as experienced before was seen as raw, profane, and damned; now that the missionaries had arrived, real life had begun. God, they said, had not visited Africa before; it was the missionaries' task to introduce Africans to the Creator God. And in spite of the way Africans lived out their daily lives in constant celebration of their spiritual encounters with God, little respect was given to their deep-rooted religious life.

Traditional African rituals of conception, birth, naming, passage, age groups, marriage, healing, harvest, thanksgiving, chieftaincy, dedication, welcoming, travel, funerals, the final or second burials, and the memorial of ancestors were some of the ways traditional Africans celebrated the communion between humanity and divinity. All these, however, were, in the

17

name of the Lord, swept away by the missionaries as pagan and unspiritual. Along with them also went village shrines, ceremonial costumes, local drums, and many other musical instruments, as well as traditional healers, ministers, and prophets. To embrace the Catholic faith, one was expected virtually to deny self and history, learn to be European in one's thinking, curse the past, and be baptized.

Those who condemned the African drums and gongs and xylophones brought along organs and foreign-made flutes and brass band instruments. Only those instruments imported from abroad were considered worthy to be used in the worship of the Lord. Suddenly, the God Africans had served and worshiped for centuries — since long before anyone walked the European lands — stopped hearing the people's language and music. The people could no longer offer fruits from their harvests or wine from their palm or banana trees; now they had to buy their offerings from faraway America and Europe.

However positively motivated they were, the missionaries could not see that even within Christian practice itself there have always existed elements similar to what they wanted to eradicate in Africa. A large cathedral is no more a shrine dedicated to God than a small mud house in the village square where the people gather to celebrate and give thanks to the Creator God. The pipe organ assembled in England and the African drum both serve their historical and musical purposes. Nor is grape wine from Portugal more sacred than palm wine from Nigeria.

The missionaries preached that they were the ones who established the relationship between God and the people, that in all cases their presence compensated for anybody else who might be absent. Missionaries baptized infants in the presence of only the parents; they did not require an assembly of a wider group. Anointings often took place in secret. Reconciliation took place in secret and in private. Marriage was

performed with the priest and the couple (and church practice sometimes permits marriage to take place even when one
of those to be married is absent). Many of these practices
seemed strange to the Africans called to the Catholic faith, but
there was no room for asking questions. Even the elders in the
village could not raise any objections when Christian practice
appeared to insult the traditions of the people.

Missionary work in those early days had its risks, but it
also had a lot of power attached to it. The risk involved disease, local hostility on the part of some, interreligious conflict,
diet, loneliness, and language difficulties. The missionaries
were compensated by the overwhelming respect and hospitality they experienced among many African people. As a little
boy growing up in West Africa, I saw our parents and grand-
parents buying eggs weekly to be given to the missionary at
every Sunday Eucharist. Our family then served eggs only a
few times a year, at Christmas and on other major feast days.
We thought that the Irish missionaries did not even use toilet
facilities; somehow they were supposed to have transcended
such natural activities.

In that experience God was pushed further away from the
people and made very abstract. European dualism and class
distinctions were brought in, thus distorting the unified sense
of nature as understood by Africans. Individualism began to
be promoted at the cost of community and extended family
spirit. Then there followed the negation of the importance of
the assembly, a disrespect for the music and the dance of the
people, the rhythm and the rituals, the colors and the beauty
of nature. The power of the spoken word was undermined.
Healing was set aside. And although there were thousands of
baptisms every week and the church's statistical success was
great, the quality of the evangelization is questionable.

Appreciating African Values

I don't want only to blame the missionaries, however. Indeed many Africans today, notwithstanding their African birthright and the immense theological education of some, placed in positions of ministerial authority themselves look down on the spiritual and cultural heritage of their people. So why should we expect Irishmen to have put aside their cassocks and their cigars and jumped into the dancing circles of the African villages and stamped their feet into the African sands to the rhythm of African drums and gongs?

Most African priests, religious, and bishops today would not consider themselves called to sing and dance unto the Lord at the Sunday celebration. The education received in seminaries and formation houses has systematically alienated us from our African heritage. Consequently, many of our African ministers are far more closed to the idea of incarnating the liturgy than our foreign-born collaborators. In recent years, I have seen many white European and American priests, bishops, and nuns who, moved by the musical sounds and vibrations of the African drums and instruments at the Sunday celebration, loosen up and break into rhythmic movement and dance. And I have seen this happen more often than I have seen it among African church ministers. The problem is not with Africans but with the formation and educational programs received in seminaries and convents.

There were also missionaries who were open to the Spirit in recognizing the beauty and grace of African life. Some founders of missionary groups offered sound advice to those that they sent out. Francis Libermann, the founder of the Holy Ghost Fathers, advised the people he sent to the missions not to preach Europe but the gospel of Jesus the Christ and to leave intact aspects of the people's lives that radiate the grace of God. Another missionary, Placide Tempels, through his studies and writings has helped even Africans themselves to a fuller understanding of traditional life and religion. Many missionaries dedicated their time and talents to educational and health-care ministries. Through the establishment of schools, missionaries played an important role in the formation of the new African nations' first leaders. Through mission hospitals, missionaries provided new hope and life to many Africans who would otherwise have died prematurely.

Another beautiful example of positive missionary input is the founder of the contemplative convent of St. Damian in Sangmelima, Cameroon, who symbolizes the exemplary sensitive missionary. A former missionary to Asia from France, Mother Mary of Jesus went to Africa to help Africans discover a contemplative way of life suited to their environment. Her goals were specific: the development of an Afro-Christian monastic life. In the face of local resistance to monastic life, she had tremendous success. Within about ten years, her African congregation had seventy nuns. What is of interest to us, however, is not the size of her congregation but the way she related to African life. When asked to explain her success, she said:

> I believe that Africans are predisposed toward a contemplative life. The African soul, which is very religious, is constantly in dialogue with things invisible. When touched by the supernatural, or the mysterious, its sensibility allows it to vibrate like the strings of a harp. Then the customs of village life are themselves the raw material of monastic life. If so many other experiments [in the monastic life] have failed, it is because people have thought it necessary to Europeanize or Americanize African men and women. After a few years, the Africans feel the longing of their own personality, and they leave. Here [in her community], young women have been able

to express their contemplative souls freely. I have only helped them to find themselves by leading a family life with them, making them tell the legends of their villages, their fears, the things that were forbidden them, everything that has left a mark on their childhood. This has set them free, and allows them to discern the things which are valuable in African life in order that they may preserve them. Thus we have found that dancing in the liturgy is a very valuable expression for the African religious woman. The African is a very rhythmic being who translates his entire life into dance, from the cradle to the grave. Should we exclude it from the religious life and worship? The young novices have spontaneously found rhythmic gestures and songs which express their prayers. They have perfected, purified, sanctified them, and finally considered them worthy of inclusion in the liturgy. For each Sunday, they compose a new dance; it is a continual process. And visitors are surprised to discover a complete prayer in which the whole being, body, as well as soul, returns to God.[3]

Mother Mary of Jesus listened to the yearnings of the African soul in developing a style of African monastic life. She knew that before Christianity arrived in Africa, God had already made an alliance with African peoples. Missionaries had only to recognize at the outset of their ministries that God has already visited the people. As an Ashanti proverb says, "Wood already touched by fire is not hard to light."

By and large, however, Africans themselves were coming to the conclusion that most of the missionaries had a different philosophy of the human person. The missionaries assumed that the Africans that they were addressing employed the same thought categories as themselves and should consequently understand the symbols they employed. The result was the juxtaposition of different systems, eventually leading to what Ralph E. Tanner has referred to as "a working misunderstanding."[4] For instance, the distinctions between spirit and body, sacred and profane, invisible and visible, were very prevalent in the philosophy of the missionaries. In line with the theology of their homelands they considered liturgy to be a spiritual activity.

One of the fundamental problems faced by the missionaries concerned communication. African languages are quite different from those of the evangelizers. The initial attitude of the missionaries showed some insensitivity to these basic differences; many equated the ability to speak a native language with the ability to decode its system of expression. It took the missionaries a century of presence in the heartland of Africa before they finally realized that behind every African word or expression lies a network of sentiments and meanings that are not easily communicable in speech. A veteran missionary to Zaire wrote:

> There are quite a few of us who master the language relatively well, but the "emotional" value of the language escapes us almost completely. Some words and expressions have an entirely different intellectual-emotional content for the native Bantu than for us. The longer one has lived in Africa, the more one questions what words like "love," "God," "evil spirit," "evil," and "sin" mean. The older and wiser one becomes, the more he is aware that there are two worlds that have many similarities, but also many opposite poles. Born in a country with a Christian cultural background, with a Western mentality and culture, we are fond of logical approaches. To us, work is almost more important than life; we want to realize, to create something, but we lack resignation and self-reflection.[5]

Many missionaries neither appreciated nor understood the African sense of the primacy of the human body and its uses in the cultic life. So they condemned traditional religious music and dances in African worship. Blind to the role of the woman in African society and ignorant of the matriarchal systems that organize the life and activity of many African clans (for example, the Ashanti people of Ghana), they insisted that liturgical ministries, even participation in the choir, be the prerogative of the men. Sadly enough, because they regarded African music as "pagan," the music and musical instruments that they allowed in the Christian assembly were limited to Gregorian chant and the organ. When anything of the local culture was used, for example, the vernacular in singing, the melody was borrowed from some Latin hymn or some other song originating in medieval Europe. In the words of Bishop Anselme Sanon, the Christian liturgy that we inherited has neither feet nor arms; it is all spirit and no body. It has tried to be from everywhere and succeeds in being from nowhere; it cries out aloud to be given a humanity through its contact with the African world.[6]

Project of African Christianity

Five years after the end of the Second Vatican Council, liturgical adaptation directed by missionaries in Africa was still crippled. It had proceeded no further than verbal translation and the toleration of local melodies and gestures to enhance the translated words.

History was made in 1969 when Pope Paul VI visited Africa. During his visit to Kampala, Uganda, the pope's address to the assembly of African bishops made headlines and brought African bishops and theologians to their feet. Among other things, the pope said to the bishops:

The expression, that is, the language and mode of manifesting this one faith, may be manifold, hence it may be original, suited to the tongue, the style, the character, the genius and the culture of the one who professes this one faith. From this point of view, a certain pluralism is not only legitimate, but desirable. An adaptation of the Christian life in the fields of pastoral, ritual, didactic and spiritual activities is not only possible, it is even favored by the church. The liturgical renewal is a living example of this. And in this sense, *you may, and you must have an African Christianity. Indeed you possess human values and characteristic forms of culture which can rise up to perfection so as to find in Christianity, and for Christianity, a true superior fullness and prove to be capable of a richness of expression all its own, and genuinely African* [emphasis added]. You have the strength and the grace necessary for this, because you are living members of the Catholic Church, because you are Christians and you are Africans.[7]

The words "you may, and you must have an African Christianity" became the theme of the assembly of theologians who gathered in Abidjan, Ivory Coast, the following year. From then on, the papal affirmation that Africans have human values from which the church could benefit opened a new chapter in the relationship between Christianity and African peoples with their traditional religion.

With much respect for what had been written and said before that date, one must concede that it was that speech of Paul VI in 1969 that acted as the immediate source of inspiration for many local churches of Africa to rise to their feet and celebrate their gifts. In the church of Zaire, that same energy was translated into life when the bishops conference there gave birth to a historic liturgical proposal. The

bishops asked their Commission on Evangelization to propose a eucharistic liturgy better suited to the genius of their
people. On the basis of the commission's groundwork, the
bishops conference presented a schema for the new rite on
December 4, 1969, and requested permission from Rome to
develop it. The permission was granted. From then on, that
local church took up the challenge that had been addressed
to Africa: to become its own missionary and to construct an
African Christianity.

At the Roman Synod of 1974, the theme of which was
"Evangelization," the bishops of Africa and Madagascar officially challenged the "theology of adaptation" and opted
instead for what they called the "theology of incarnation." Part
of their declaration stated:

> Our theological thinking must remain faithful to the au-
> thentic tradition of the church and, at the same time, be
> attentive to the life of our communities and respectful
> of our traditions and languages, that is, of our philoso-
> phy of life. Following this idea of mission, *the Bishops of
> Africa and Madagascar consider as being completely out-of-
> date, the so-called theology of adaptation. In its stead, they
> adopt the theology of incarnation* [emphasis added]. The
> young churches of Africa and Madagascar cannot refuse
> to face up to this basic demand. They accept the fact of
> theological pluralism within the unity of faith, and con-
> sequently they must encourage, by all means, African
> theological research. Theology must be open to the aspi-
> ration of the people of Africa, if it is to help Christianity
> to become incarnate in the life of the peoples of the Af-
> rican continent. To achieve this, the young churches of
> Africa and Madagascar must take over more and more
> responsibility for their own evangelization and total de-
> velopment. They must combine creativity with dynamic

responsibility.... The grave problems of the hour and the very nature of the church itself, the Body of Christ, make this imperative.[8]

The above statement was a clear manifestation of discontent with missionary Christianity. It was a judgment whose time had come. In fact, it was a judgment not only on the missionaries who came and worked in Africa, but also on those members of the Vatican Congregations who had never been in Africa, but who claimed the prerogative of knowing how Africans should worship the living God. Those who spoke from Rome were popularly regarded as "missionaries who have not yet come." The question then raised in Africa was not only about what missionaries were doing, but also what rules and norms were being imposed from the Holy See. The African church was coming of age.

The process of preparing for the 1974 Synod of Bishops had raised questions that unsettled many a missionary on the African continent. It was to calm that anxiety that various conferences of bishops issued statements to acknowledge the good works of the missionaries and to invite them to be collaborators in the new task of advancing the work they had already begun. In an address to foreign missionaries in their country, the Zairean bishops asked them to become listeners and to learn to be assimilated into the environment. They did not have to fear being sent away now that leadership had entered into the hands of indigenous clergy. They should rather be constantly aware of the lines of conduct already set out by the bishops conference.

Most important, however, has been the strength of faith and vivacity of character of the Zairean Catholics who, with over 60 percent of the population of the country, proportionately constitute one of the largest percentages of Catholics among African countries.

Closely related to the theology of incarnation is the notion of "inculturation." Since the term first appeared in theological circles a few years before the opening of the Second Vatican Council, it has spread in its use and appeal throughout the world church. Its genesis was related to aspects of evangelization and Christian witnessing in the young churches (usually called the "missions"). With time, "inculturation" replaced the term "adaptation" used by the Vatican II documents, especially with regard to Christian liturgy in various cultures of the world. Under the term "adaptation," it was enough to take the Roman Missal to any culture and ask the local bishops to use it in such a way as to make it understood by the people (without, of course, changing the structure or essential content). The concept of adaptation served as a stepping stone for greater outreach to the cultures and value systems of non-European Catholics around the world. The dominant cultures of Europe, for long promoted by European missionaries as they went about evangelizing in foreign countries, were making it difficult for people to separate the gospel from Euroculture. Church leaders in Africa pushed very hard to have the emerging concept of inculturation supersede the crippling concept of adaptation.

Although not spoken of explicitly in any document of Vatican II, inculturation had become increasingly important by the late 1970s. It requires theological alertness to the data of a cultural milieu; it is a creative and powerful method of evangelization; it fosters an awakening to the diverse riches of the world's cultures; it dynamically gives birth to new dimensions in the celebration of the Christian mystery. Supported by the powerful concept of incarnation, taken from the divine method that is our ultimate model, the term "inculturation" began to appear in official church documents. The 1985 Extraordinary Synod in Rome said in this regard:

Since the church is a communion which joins diversity and unity, being present throughout the world, it takes up whatever it finds positive in all cultures. Inculturation, however, is different from a mere external adaptation, as it signifies an interior transformation of authentic cultural values through integration into christianity and the rooting of christianity in various human cultures.[9]

Liturgical inculturation is the process whereby a local church, rooted in the truth of its cultural, spiritual, political, economic, and social uniqueness, strives to celebrate life in Jesus Christ within the context of life as lived in community. There are three players here: first, the people of the community; second, their way of life; and third, the gospel of Jesus the Christ. There is a reason for placing them in this order, namely, our ordinary human experience: we are first born as human beings, into a culture; the initiation into the Christian community follows. This initiation can never erase the human person or the cultural situation but, instead, builds on them through grace.

Important for the evolution of the Zairean Mass to its present form were the contributions of Zairean bishops and theologians concerning this whole issue of inculturation. The presence, initiative, and leadership of these theologians as well as the dynamism and research orientations of the theological institutions in Kinshasa played a most important role in the process. In the meantime, there were also some serious anthropological studies done of African life and religion that helped to deepen appreciation of African religion. With that reflection and search in progress, a greater awareness of what should make up an African liturgy was gained. The Belgian origin of most of the missionaries in Zaire was also significant because of the Belgian contributions to the liturgical movement prior to Vatican II. The "national authenticity" movement in Zaire, beginning in the early 1970s, also played an important role, as did the general trend in Africa toward the development of African philosophy and African theology, a movement that attracted the participation of theologians and liturgists across the African continent.

Chapter 2

A New Eucharistic Celebration Born in Africa

Zaire is located in the central region of the African continent. Previously known as the Belgian Congo, Zaire is one of the largest countries of Africa, geographically speaking, with an estimated population of 35 million. Political independence from Belgium was celebrated on June 30, 1960. It was on that occasion that Patrice Lumumba, then leader of the Congo people, proposed to make a model of that country. "We are going to show the world what the black man can do when he works in freedom, and we are going to make the Congo the center of radiance for the whole of Africa." In some ways, that dream has come true. Zairean music has permeated all of Africa, successfully tying together the various musical styles of the entire continent. As many have said, the entire African continent sings and dances to Zairean melodies.

Early missionary work in Zaire was very successful, or at least so it seemed. Christianity grew rapidly in the region because of the cooperation between the colonial government and the church. But as in many parts of the continent, missionaries were yet to learn that the pouring of water and a change of name are not enough to guarantee true Christian initiation.

As the Second Vatican Council was being concluded, Zaire was entering one of the most troubling moments in its history. On November 25, 1965, Lieutenant General Joseph D. Mobutu ousted both the president and the premier of the country. Taking over the executive power, he set up a one-party government. In the years that followed, Mobutu, then a practicing Catholic, initiated open confrontations with the Catholic Church in Zaire. In his own way, he was instituting fundamental reforms for his people under the umbrella term "national authenticity." The effects of those confrontations have left lasting marks on the face of the Zairean church.

One of Mobutu's earliest actions against the church was his formal suppression of foreign names borne by Zairean citizens. He legislated that henceforth all identifications in the country had to be made with local names and designations. He himself dropped his former names, Joseph Désiré, and took up the names Mobutu Sese Seko Kuku Ngbeandu Wa Za Banga. He has since shortened the name to Mobutu Sese Seko.

Mobutu also nationalized the Catholic University of Kinshasa (then called Lovanium). Founded in 1954, it was the first Catholic university in Africa, modeled after the Catholic University of Louvain, Belgium. As a result of this government intervention, the theology department of the university in Kinshasa left the campus and reorganized itself as the Faculté de Théologie Catholique de Kinshasa. This institution, under the patronage of the bishops conference of Zaire, has grown to be the most solidly organized theological center on the African continent, producing outstanding scholars of international recognition and at the same time inspiring serious research and publications in the areas of African philosophy, theology, anthropology, spirituality, and, in a special way, liturgy. This center of research has been at the heart of any progress made in Zaire in the ongoing dialogue and in the development of the concept of inculturation in ecclesiastical circles.

Much of what will be said about the Zairean liturgy will be associated with the city of Kinshasa, which became Zaire's capital in 1927. Kinshasa has had its glorious days, but in recent years, it has been noted for economic decadence and political aberrations. There has also been devastation of human lives in Zaire due to the AIDS virus. Recently, the human tragedies in neighboring Rwanda and Burundi have flooded Zaire with refugees who need assistance that Zaire cannot give. And now the mysterious outbreak of the Ebola virus in Zaire is causing more panic and fear. These tragedies are distorting the music of the land. In spite of the constant processions of families to the graveyard to bury their loved ones, however, the neighborhoods are not devoid of music and celebration. Somehow the people of Zaire continue to hold their heads above water. It is in spiritual and cultural life that pride has survived; perhaps it is in these too that the country will find definition for its future.

The Incubation of the Zairean Rite

The church of Zaire was the first truly to address the issue of bringing African life and sense into Catholic liturgy. Well before the deliberations of the Second Vatican Council on the liturgy were begun, the bishops of Zaire were already talking about how to "adapt" the Christian liturgy to their people. In 1961, the bishops of Zaire gathered in assembly declared:

> The liturgy introduced in Africa is not yet adapted to the proper character of our populations, and therefore has remained foreign to them. The return to the authentic traditions of the liturgy greatly opens the way

to a fundamental adaptation of the liturgy to the African environment. Such an adaptation is very necessary for the edification of the traditional (pagan) community on religious grounds, since worship is the most important element that unites the entire community. Only a living and adapted form of worship can generate the indispensable deepening of the faith, which cannot be given through instruction alone....An elaborate study and critique of the religious customs as well as a living contact with the people will reveal the fundamental cultural needs and will furnish the necessary elements for the elaboration of a living African liturgy sensitive to the aspirations of the populations.[10]

The bishops had already discerned the need for a locally oriented renewal of the liturgy. Earlier on at the meeting, the bishops had said that the adaptation of the Mass in their region would necessitate the adoption of the various means of local expression: words, music, gestures, and African cultural means of communication in general. The bishops had various requests with regard to the ritual. Inspired by the decisions made at a conference on "Liturgy and the Missions" in Nijmegen in the Netherlands, the bishops asked that the use of local language be allowed in such matters as the giving of the nuptial blessing. They also asked that in view of the need to be sensitive to the local dispositions and cultural milieu, permission be given for them to formulate new prayers and adapt the rites for the celebration of the sacraments and sacramentals and to eliminate those rites that were not in accord with local sentiments. The bishops had to wait for the document on the liturgy of the Second Vatican Council for a response to their requests.

Meanwhile, by the end of their meeting in 1961, it was clear that the bishops had become very much aware of the necessity of being sensitive to their local culture. From then on, a concerted effort was made to inaugurate a local movement for the renewal of the liturgy in the region. That movement was sustained by the outcome of the discussions concerning the liturgy during the Second Vatican Council. The growing awareness of the values of traditional African life and the emerging critique of missionary Christianity gave rise to a new style of celebrating the Eucharist.

It was the church of Zaire that earlier had produced the "Missa Luba," a humble but daring attempt to use African musical instruments to accompany the Roman Mass sung in Latin. At the time of its release in the early 1960s, it was the first introduction of African rhythm, drums, and gongs into Catholic celebrations.

Shortly after the release of Vatican II's document on the liturgy in 1963, a seminar on various rites of the church, with special emphasis on the Ethiopian rite, was held in Kinshasa. The seminar helped broaden awareness of the possibility of liturgical pluralism in the Catholic Church.

The dating of the first proposal for a Zairean rite must be placed after the release of the new Roman Missal on April 3, 1969. The appearance of the Missal created reservations on the part of some African bishops. It was argued that the Missal represented the Euro-American viewpoint from which it originated. Besides, Pope Paul VI's Apostolic Constitution *Missale Romanum* of April 3, 1969, which promulgated the Missal, insisted that the new Missal could allow for only minor variations and adaptations, since it was expected to be an "instrument of liturgical unity." It is not a question here of African bishops rejecting unity with the world church, but rather that of the inadequacy of the new Missal with regard to African cultural and religious values. Nowhere was that reservation better expressed in Africa than in Zaire. The bishops had maintained earlier that to Africanize the liturgy does not mean merely to adopt some customs usual in the African cultural context; rather it means to create a liturgy that incarnates the message of revelation in a specific socio-cultural context, thus presenting the mystery celebrated by the Christian community in an expressive and comprehensive manner. It is therefore not enough for the liturgy to be Zairean; it must also be Christian. A commission was set up to work on the new liturgy.

The Task before the Diocesan Liturgical Commission

The challenge facing the commission was enormous, since it had to battle with two imposing extremes: on the one hand, a loyal and uncritical inclination to maintain the renewed Roman rite, and on the other hand, an unreflective return to and a nostalgic embrace of the ancestral cults of the villages. The task was clearly described in the following assessment of liturgical life in Zaire before the new Mass was born.

> After a century of Roman liturgy, there are quite a few prominent African Catholics who don't want to part with the old Latin and the Gregorian chant. Many of them are alumni of our seminaries and boarding schools who are very familiar with all the peculiarities of rubrics and Gregorian chant. In Kinshasa particularly, most of the Masses for the deceased are requested with a "demand" that the Mass be offered in Latin.... There is another and more difficult problem related to the great number of different tribes who make up the population of Kinshasa. And it's not just the language that creates the problem. Tribes differ in ways of expressing their feelings and emotions. What is accepted as a very dignified and adequate expression of joy or sorrow in one tribe

looks silly and ridiculous to another. To find the common elements which will be accepted by all Congolese will be either impossible or very impractical because by doing so we may again take all life out of a Congolese liturgy. We know that we must rely on the Congolese priests and educated laity to do this work. They however, are by education and training also estranged from their own people;... they must re-establish contact with their own people. Even that may prove to be impossible in a metropolis like Kinshasa because Congolese society is undergoing deep changes not only in the local centers, but particularly and primarily in the large urban areas. Since Independence day, the "city" has been opened to all foreign elements.... Society as a whole is in a ferment and the Congolese is more and more developing toward the universal prototype.... The great problem then is that the church may well make giant efforts to adapt its liturgy and consequently its religious education system to a society that no longer exists. The church will have to be very careful not to cling to elements which already are folklore. It will take more than a casual study to find out what in the Congolese soul are proper and everlasting values.[11]

The commission's initial goal was to marry the Christian genius with African life. At that time, the commission accepted the new Roman *Ordo* as an adequate representation of the Christian genius. With the people of Zaire already awaiting the introduction of their new rite, it was felt that the Roman *Ordo* provided the best starting point for developing a new rite for Zaire. To arrive at a determination of the African genius to be incorporated into the celebration of the Eucharist, the commission focused on the role of the presider and asked the question: "How does a chief act or what does he do when he presides at the town meeting?" It was supposed that the role of the presider at the Eucharist would mirror the role of the chief in the village assembly. Highlighting the role of the chief/presider led the diocesan commissions to reflect upon the structure of their local village assemblies. The question was this: how would a chief authentically immersed in African tradition best bear witness to the mystery of Christ?

In the development of the Zairean Mass, three models have had an influence on the composition and celebration. Rome asked for the use of the Roman *Ordo Missae* as a starting point. The Zairean commission took the model of the tribal chief, centering its considerations on the actions of the priest-presider. There also appears an African model of assembly within a kinship. We will consider each of these and the resulting amalgam of the three, as well as the influence of the actual celebration on what has evolved.

The Model of the Roman Order of the Mass

When it gave its permission to the Zairean bishops for the development of the new Zairean Mass, the Vatican Congregation for Divine Worship offered the *Ordo* of the Roman Mass as the point of departure for the Zairean liturgical commission. The Congregation asked that the *Ordo* be integrated into Zairean life. The people of Zaire were thus asked to start with an already-made product imported from the northern hemisphere, whose characteristics were mostly alien to them. This constituted an initial problem for authentic African expression in the eucharistic celebration.

That the Roman Congregation imposed the *Ordo* on the commission for this kind of pioneering work is not surprising, especially when we recall the time when the permission was sought. What is surprising is that the bishops, having set out to develop a eucharistic liturgy that is truly Christian and truly African (or, more specifically, truly "congolais"), would bow to the imposition of the *Ordo* as the inalienable point of departure. Beginning with the *Ordo* was one of the flaws of the work of the Zairean liturgical commission. According to a Catholic missionary and liturgical consultant in Zaire, Boniface Luykx, who himself did not support that point of departure, the commission could have begun with the studies already made concerning ancient eucharistic rites in view of developing an African rite of the Eucharist.

A respected Nigerian theologian and liturgist, Elochukwu Uzukwu, who has demonstrated great interest in the Zairean project, wrote that the Zairean commission should have taken a different direction to create for itself a wider scope for interpreting the Christian tradition.

> [The commission] could have taken the New Testament Lord's Supper (Paul), or Breaking of the bread (Luke), as the norm for what must be considered central to a Christian eucharistic celebration. Then it should have scrutinized the variety of liturgical texts of the patristic period as indications of how each cultural group (or rather local church) could shape its expression of the core of the eucharistic celebration. Finally, it should have been on guard against medieval decadence which exalted the individual over against the communitarian, the clergy over against the faithful, devotional idiosyncrasies over against the paschal mystery.[12]

This criticism should be read in conjunction with what Uzukwu says concerning sensitivity not only to the church's tradition, but also to African life and in this case especially African ritual meals:

> The Zairean liturgical experiment would meet our idea of an inculturated African eucharistic celebration if it

projects a Christian celebration which expresses joyously salvation from God in the Christ in a cultic meal-setting, and if it takes seriously assemblies and meal celebrations practiced in the traditional African experience of God, ancestors, spirits, and forces. The celebration would thus express how the African tradition is now under the transforming direction of the Christ whom African Christians confess as savior. Thus in the Zairean rite one should expect a necessary freedom to express the transforming effect of God's salvific work in Zairean tradition which only Zaireans can truly and deeply experience. In addition, one should anticipate the dialectics of acceptance and rejection as the necessary consequence of the transforming action of God among African peoples to bring about in the Christ a new creation.[13]

On the positive side, the use of the *Ordo* provided the commission an "acceptable" point of departure for their work. Not only did they have a common ground for dialogue with Rome; they also were provided with themes that belong to the long tradition of eucharistic practice.

On the negative side, however, as a result of accepting the Roman *Ordo* as starting point, the commission had to take the present constituent parts of the Roman Mass as indispensable parts of the eucharistic celebration. But the *Ordo*, despite the purging during the revision, still possesses elements of medieval piety that do not have to be imposed on the young churches of today as indispensable elements of the liturgy.

Any model proposed for an African liturgy that does not express the genius of African life, African values, and their symbolic expressions, ought to be rejected as an inadequate point of departure. The Roman *Ordo* was not composed with the African world in view.

The Model of the Chief

The initial guidelines used by the commission for working out the celebration of the liturgy were based on what the chief did in the village assembly. The actions of the priest rather than those of the assembly were highlighted by the commission. This model of the presider was to be used alongside the prescriptions of the Roman *Ordo*. By highlighting the role of the presider, the Zairean commission ran the risk of dwarfing the role of the assembly and confirming a strongly hierarchical theology of the priesthood. Vatican II, on the other hand, had called for a revival of the Christian celebration as a community action, with great importance attached to the participation of the faithful. This includes the development of liturgical ministries for the laity.

An example of a potentially adverse effect of the village chief model involves the lector's request for a blessing before the reading. If the emphasis is on passing on the authority to speak at the assembly, it promotes clericalism and diminishes the sense of the priesthood of the baptized. On the other hand, if the emphasis is on asking and receiving blessing for a fruitful ministry to the worshiping assembly, this practice can have a much richer and deeper importance.

With the model of the chief, the presider is invested with so much authority that the celebration becomes a reflection of the authoritarian leadership that Zaire and other African countries experienced in the past and still do under some African political leaders. There is, of course, a trend in the church today that continues to emphasize a hierarchical Christian ministry, thus elevating the ordained priesthood far above the other ministries. Is this not one area in which the gospel can offer some form of liberation?

The Model of the African Assembly

The Zairean commission was quick to moderate its hierarchical view of the eucharistic assembly. The commission's understanding was influenced by African rituals involving the ancestors and spirits of the African world, and thus the celebration found deep expressions of joy, color, gesture, and dance. The model of the presiding African chief, while it retained some form of the sovereignty of the chief, was enlarged to incorporate the African values of family and community, thus involving the active participation of the people. The role of the presider was no longer the focus; the reference became the assembly itself.

This expanded model is very close to the spirit of Vatican II's notion of "full, conscious, active participation of the faithful demanded by the very nature of the liturgy." Traditional African celebrations, whether for marriages or funerals or other forms of initiation, are accompanied by rituals associated with the model of the assembly. This model is not to be confused with "laissez-faire" or anarchy. While there is internal order built into such an assembly through its leadership, much accent is given to the role of the people. The sense of community and family forms the basis for active participation in worship.

The Zairean Mass: A Melding of Models

In taking the Roman *Ordo Missae* as its point of departure, the commission considered the various components of the celebration: entrance procession, kissing the altar, greeting the people, penitential rituals, readings, bringing of gifts, eucharistic prayer, sign of peace, breaking of bread and sharing of the eucharistic elements, blessing, sending forth, and the regular prayers of the Eucharist. It was the aim of the commission to find a culturally sensitive expression for each of the parts of the Mass, whether in word or in gesture. The chief, that is, the presider at the Eucharist, would have to use African idioms that are expressive of the Christian message.

In its adaptation of the Roman celebration, the commission made only a few structural changes that reflect African cultural and religious values, changes that will be considered below. Dealing with a number of models at the same time can be a very difficult method. The Zairean commission should be given credit for being able to draw some form of synthesis from virtually independent models. By so doing, they claimed their place in the mainstream of the church's liturgical tradition, at the same time drawing attention to the richness of African life.

All the same, we discern in this process a problem of *methodology*. The insertion of African ideas and symbols into the Roman liturgy does not give birth to an authentic African liturgy, any more than an American could become African by eating an African dish or by wearing an African dress. The process has resulted in an *elongation* of the liturgy because of appendages and elaborations. By extensively stitching African ideas into the Roman liturgy, the Zairean Mass today holds the title to the continent's longest Catholic celebration of the Eucharist, usually exceeding two hours in length. I have no problem with the length of the celebration, however; rather it is the content and quality of celebration that is of concern. For example, the Zairean Mass takes up Eucharistic Prayer II of the Roman Sacramentary, adds some African themes, introduces some responses, and modifies some concepts, but avoids any radical creativity. This liturgy remains Roman in spirit.

Theologians in Africa who have composed eucharistic prayers or have participated in the development of a complete eucharistic celebration have so far remained close to the structure, spirit, and even the rubrics of the Roman Sacramentary. For instance, although these theologians may be convinced that they speak for people of an oral tradition, they have not raised questions about the wisdom of calling for three readings when people gather for Sunday worship, all because the Roman church wants a further exposure of the people to the Bible. Another example is bowing to Roman pressure to mix the water and the wine at the altar in front of the people. Adulterating wine before the public violates African meal ethics. Wine-tappers add water to newly tapped strong wine before it is brought out to the people.

The text of the liturgical project was published by the Zairean Episcopal Commission on Evangelization in 1974. By that time, the text had been carefully structured. According to this text, three basic criteria had been followed in the project: fidelity to gospel values, fidelity to the nature of the liturgy itself, and fidelity to the religious genius and cultural heritage of the Zairean people. These criteria can also be discerned in the basic documents that the commission worked with. The bishops noted that the commission was expected to respect the basic structures of the Catholic liturgy, to use the Roman Order of the Mass of 1969 as its basic text, to seek inspiration from the Eastern liturgies, and to introduce Zairean cultural values into the liturgy. The bishops also indicated that the Zairean Mass was to be an adaptation that respected the kerygmatic character of the liturgy of the Word and the structure of the eucharistic prayer inherited from Judaism.

Since 1974 not much has changed in the structure and content of the rite. There have been changes, however, in the style of celebration. Between 1975 and 1985, while correspondence continued between Rome and Zaire with regard to final approvals, there was increased incorporation of local music and musical instruments and local art, dance, rhythm, and costume, as well as greater use of dialogue in the celebration. The model of the gathering of the assembly was superseding the model of the village chief as presider.

In the course of the many meetings, exchanges of correspondence, and dialogues between the Zairean church and Rome, everybody learned. The following demands of the Vatican authorities were accepted by the Zairean side: to distinguish clearly the roles of the announcer and the deacon and to describe their respective roles in the text, to modify or eliminate certain "unfortunate" passages aimed at theological insight about ancestors, to include the texts of the Gloria and the Credo, to include a homily, and to maintain the traditional words of the institution narrative. On the other hand, the Zairean side successfully held its ground (with reasons acceptable to the Vatican authorities) against the demand to begin the invocation of saints and ancestors with the traditional Roman formula "Kyrie eleison." They also insisted on allowing the presiders to have the choice of where in the Mass to have the penitential rite and the kiss of peace (that is, either as in the Roman Mass or as in the Zairean text). Finally, on the issue of mixing the water and wine before the offertory procession the Vatican authorities did not accept the explanations made.

While the Zairean bishops used the term "inculturation" to describe what they were attempting to accomplish, Rome found it more opportune to use "acculturation" and "adaptation." At the same time, while the Zairean bishops wanted to identify the uniqueness of Christian cultic experience in their local churches, the Roman delegation kept reminding them of Pope John Paul II's demand during his apostolic visits to Africa for sensitivity toward the unity of the world church.

During the negotiations, however, one underlying message kept emerging: Rome cannot today close the doors that were opened at Vatican II.

A Celebration of Ritual Recognition

No matter how long the night, the day is sure to come. On April 23, 1988, several bishops of Zaire were received in audience in Rome by John Paul II during their "ad limina" visit. In his address to the pope, Cardinal Joseph Malula indicated how the Zairean church had continued "along the path drawn by the Council." At the top of the list of primary concerns of their church was the project of inculturation, and here he specifically made reference to the Zairean liturgical project:

> The major project of liturgical inculturation, how well completed, concerns the proper manner for celebrating the Eucharist. The Zairean church shall be glad to give this work as an offering to the Catholic tradition. The long process of its elaboration has been an exemplary experience of dialogue between the Holy See and a particular church. We wish to seize this opportunity to thank the Apostolic See for the encouragement and support received throughout the period, as we now await the final approval of your Holiness at an opportune time.[14]

Then the cardinal committed the church in Zaire to the elaboration and inculturation of the rituals of the other sacraments, outlining briefly how this would be achieved through collaboration between the bishops and the theological expertise readily available in Kinshasa.

In his reply, the pope acknowledged how the Zairean church had received him warmly during his 1980 and 1985 visits. Mentioning that he had received their "concerns" sent the previous year, he simply indicated that he had those concerns at heart. With reference to the celebration of the Eucharist, the pope said that the present form, which was still "ad experimentum," demanded further examination as well as some refinement. He then praised the dialogue that had occurred during the entire process and hoped that it would continue for the elaboration of other rituals.

On April 30, 1988, just one week after the pope's meeting with the bishops, the Congregation for Divine Worship gave the formal approval of the Zairean rite of the Eucharist with the official title "Missel Romain pour les Dioceses du Zaire" (Roman Missal for the Dioceses of Zaire). The Zairean church did not propose this title, nor is the title well accepted in Zaire. The title was suggested and forced on the Zairean church by the Roman Congregation for the Doctrine of the Faith. "Rite Zairois" (Zairean rite) is what is heard in Zaire today.

Chapter 3

Description of the Zairean Eucharist

To better appreciate the approved text of the Zairean Mass, it will be helpful at this point to look at the initial proposal put forth by the diocesan Commission on Evangelization. Since the internal structure of that first proposal does not differ much from that contained in the Order of the Roman liturgy, our emphasis here will be centered on the initial signs of innovations in the Zairean Mass.

The Initial Proposal

The description that follows is restricted to the first part of the liturgy, up to and including the presentation of gifts, since it is only in this first part that innovations were projected.

The internal format of the celebration is envisioned as similar to that of a village assembly or a popular town meeting, with people in a festive mood. The liturgy is celebrated Sunday morning or evening. The people assemble in church and take their places. The men and women appointed to special ministries during the celebration wear vestments of native African prints, usually in accord with the liturgical color of the day. When all is ready, an "announcer" carrying a gong, a wooden drum, or some other musical instrument appears in front of the assembly, beats the instrument several times to call for the people's attention, greets the people, and announces that the celebration is about to begin. He then introduces the main ministers for the celebration and invites the assembly to rise and welcome the procession while joining in the opening song.

The procession begins at the back of the church. Included in it are all the ministers for the celebration, with each carrying his or her "staff of office." In Kinshasa the presider wears a hat made of goatskin and carries a horse tail, both symbols of royalty and power. The procession dances to the rhythm of the song. Arriving in front of the altar, the presider bows to it and places his staff on it from outside the rail without stepping into the sanctuary. No one enters the sanctuary as yet, since there will be a ritual of purification prior to such entrance.

When the song ends, the presider greets the people, introduces the day's celebration, and invites the people to join him in an opening prayer. Then he invites the people to a rite of penance. The presider may then prostrate himself, bow low, or take some other appropriate position; the people themselves take a similar position of sorrow in silence, as a tam-tam sounds at intervals in the background. When the presider rises, he recites the penitential formula (with the Kyrie) in dialogue with the people. The absolution may be a simple proclamation of the formula or a more solemn one in which the presider goes through the assembly, with the people still prostrated or bowed low, and sprinkles them with holy water, while repeating the concluding formula of pardon ("May Almighty God have mercy on us, forgive us our sins, and bring us to life everlasting"). This is followed by the mutual exchange of the kiss of peace to symbolize the reconciliation of the people among themselves.

Reconciliation is followed by the singing of the Gloria (or some other song of praise) as a sign of gratitude for having been made right again with God and neighbor. In this way, the Gloria is made part of the penitential rite, which is different from its role in the Roman liturgy. Having been cleansed too, the presider, who until now has remained in the assembly space, finally enters the sanctuary, kisses the altar, and takes his place. Like the other worshipers he too is a sinner and needed to be washed clean through the prayers of the assembly.

The liturgy of the Word follows, with the readers leading a brief invitational and responsorial dialogue with the people before and after the readings. There is a solemn procession of the book of the gospel. While the Alleluia is being sung, all those in the sanctuary form a procession; the presider takes the book, lifts it up, moves around the altar, and presents it to the people saying: "Here is the Word of God!" The people respond with applause or acclamation. The presider prays silently as the procession gradually moves to the ambo. The reading of the gospel is followed by a homily in which the preacher invites the people to responsorial participation. After that follow the Creed and the prayer of the faithful.

Two forms of the preparation of gifts are proposed. In the simple form, those bringing the gifts dance to the rhythm of the song of offering until they arrive before the altar where the presider awaits them. Then the singing stops, and the bearers ask the presider to bless them, after which they place the gifts on the credence table and return to their places. The celebration then continues as usual.

In the solemn form, those to bring the gifts wait with them (livestock, foods, bread, wine, water, and any other gifts of the people) at the entrance of the church. The presider and acolytes process to the rhythm of a song to meet them at the entrance. The assembly turns toward the door to witness what follows. Singing stops. Blessing is sought and given as in the simple form. Then the procession of presider, acolytes, and gift-bearers moves toward the altar, amid song, dance, cheering, and the assembly's gradual turning around toward the altar. The livestock is put outside. Then the celebration continues as usual when the procession arrives at the altar.

It is noteworthy that the commission did not initially plan to develop a new eucharistic prayer, but simply to adopt the short eucharistic prayer of the Roman Sacramentary with the hope of introducing responsorial segments for the people's participation.

Thus the main structural arrangement of the initial proposal can be outlined as follows:

- Procession
- Opening prayer
- Penitential rite
- Kiss of peace
- Gloria
- Entrance to the sanctuary
- Liturgy of the Word
- Presentation of gifts in procession
- Liturgy of the Eucharist
- Dismissal and recession

Innovative features include the solemn offertory rite, the position of the kiss of peace, the use of African dress and insignia, the processions with music and dance, and the role of the announcer. This was a humble beginning, but we can begin to see cultural and theological positions that stand out as independent of the Roman Mass.

The Approved Text of 1988

The text of the liturgy approved in 1988 has two main parts: the liturgy of the Word and the liturgy of the Eucharist, which are preceded by an introduction and followed by a conclusion.

The introduction includes:

- Entrance of the announcer: welcome of the assembly; invitation to worship
- Entrance procession of the presider and ministers
- Veneration of the altar
- Salutation of the people and introduction of the liturgy
- Invocation of saints and ancestors
- Song of acclamation (Gloria)
- Opening prayer

The liturgy of the Word includes:

- The first reading, responsorial psalm, and second reading
- The enthronement and proclamation of the gospel
- The homily
- Profession of faith (Credo)
- The penitential rite
- The rite/kiss of peace
- The prayer of the faithful

The liturgy of the Eucharist includes:

- Procession to the altar with the gifts
- The Eucharistic Prayer
- The Lord's Prayer
- Communion and thanksgiving
- Prayer after communion

The concluding rite includes:

- Blessing and sending forth
- Recession

Opening of the Celebration

The announcer (who is neither a priest nor a religious but who could be male or female) calls the people to worship as described earlier, but does not introduce the liturgy. The procession moves as described – in music and song and dance. The cross-bearer is usually a strong, heavily built man of the community, not a primary school pupil. Arriving at the sanctuary, the bearer of the book of the gospel places it on the altar. The presider, concelebrants, and other ministers enter the sanctuary, turn to face the people, and then together venerate the altar with a deep bow, a genuflection, or a prostration. Alternatively, while the concelebrants and ministers bow, the presider extends his hands in a V-form and kisses the four sides of the altar. This action represents the solemn embrace of the universal Christ from the four corners of the earth. Four is also a sacred number in many African regions where there are four-day weeks named after market days. At all the celebrations in which I have participated, the movement of the presider while kissing the sides of the altar has been counterclockwise. This may have to do with the African sense of ritual time: the ticking of the clock does not regulate celebration, but instead celebration regulates itself. The presider then greets the people and introduces the liturgy of the day.

Recognizing the communion that exists between the church on earth and the saints in heaven, the assembly invokes the intercession of the saints as well as the righteous ancestors in a litanic prayer. This is followed by the singing of the Gloria, during which all the ministers dance around the altar in a well-orchestrated rhythm. The ministers, who wear beautiful colored flowing robes, dance in a harmonious and reverent way around the altar while the assembly dances in its place. The presider incenses the altar and the sanctuary as he dances. The opening prayer follows, to conclude this part.

Liturgy of the Word

Before each reading, the reader bows before the presider and asks for, receives, and shows gratitude for a blessing. The sign of "showing gratitude" has to be very visible to the assembly: a reverent bow to the presider, a tapping of both hands, or a verbal expression of appreciation. The Word of God is proclaimed, and the assembly responds to each reading with an acclamation. After a procession in music, song, and dance around the altar and the enthronement of the book of the gospel, the gospel is read. The incense is also used at this time. The gospel reading is followed by a homily and the Credo.

Next is the penitential rite, here seen as response to the Word. It is a form of purification. The sprinkling of holy water and the sharing of peace (kiss of peace) follows. Depending on the region, people may wash their hands in one common basin and make the sign of the cross or shake hands with one another. The prayer of the faithful follows, during which incense may be used on a standing lighted censer.

Liturgy of the Eucharist

The presentation of gifts is made in a procession from the rear of the church; the bread and wine as well as other gifts of the people are brought forth. Representatives of the assembly present the gifts; however, the bread and wine are usually imported from abroad and are not the product of the people's land or hands. The presentation of the gifts to the priest and their reception at the altar are accompanied by the following words. The entire assembly says:

> O priest of God,
> here are our gifts.
> Receive them.
> They show our spirit of solidarity and sharing
> and that we love one another
> as the Lord has loved us.

The priest then receives and offers the gifts in the name of the community, as in the new Roman Sacramentary.

At the eucharistic prayer, the opening dialogue to the Preface is as in the Roman Sacramentary. This Preface, which is an original composition, begins with a praise of God using God's names and attributes:

> It is good that we give you thanks,
> that we glorify you,
> you, our God,
> you, our Father,
> you, the all-powerful,
> you, the sun that we cannot fix
>   our eyes upon,
> you, sight itself,
> you, the master of all peoples,
> you, the master of life,
> you, the master of all things,
> we give you thanks....

The Christological part of the Preface places a very strong emphasis on the theme of creation in Christ. There is also a vivid description of the Zairean environment, recalling how God's hand is seen in all of creation, both visible and invisible:

> He [Christ] is your word who gives life.
> Through him you created heaven and earth;

through him you created the streams of the world,
the rivers, the ponds, the lakes,
and all the fishes that dwell in them.
Through him you created the stars,
the birds of the sky, the forests,
the plains, the savannas, the mountains,
and all the animals that dwell therein.
Through him you have created all the things that we see,
and all that we do not see.

The "Holy, Holy, Holy" is sung with the ministers dancing around the altar and incensing it. The rest of the eucharistic prayer follows, with the assembly responding at various moments. This prayer, which was developed from Eucharistic Prayer II of the Roman Sacramentary, has the following parts: a pre-consecratory epiclesis (the invocation of the Holy Spirit to descend upon the people and the sacramental elements), the words of institution, the eschatological profession of the mystery of faith, the anamnesis (the memorial or remembering of the events of the life, suffering, death, and resurrection of Christ), a post-consecratory epiclesis, intercessions, and the doxology. After the eucharistic prayer, the communion rite follows.

Conclusion

The concluding rite at the end of the celebration includes the blessing and sending forth and the exit procession.

* * * * *

Note the differences between the original proposition and the approved text. In the approved text, there is an incorporation of the litany and invocation of saints and ancestors into the introductory part; the Gloria has a different meaning; the penitential rite and the kiss of peace are moved to the end of the liturgy of the Word; there is a simplification of the offertory procession; and a new eucharistic prayer is used. In the approved text, there is a more elaborate use of African images and themes. By the time of the approval, a remarkable development had occurred, not so much in the text itself as in the way the Mass was celebrated.

Structural Differences between the Roman and the Zairean Masses

A look at a comparative outline of the Roman and the Zairean liturgies reveals that their basic structures are the same: an introductory rite, the liturgy of the Word, the liturgy of the Eucharist, and a concluding rite. Within the segments, however, there are some important differences. The Zairean Mass has a more elaborate opening rite. The role of the announcer in the opening part of the liturgy is a reflection of native tradition. While this is an important characteristic of the Zairean Mass, it does not constitute a structural difference.

There are several other differences. First is the introduction of the invocation of the saints and ancestors in the introductory part of the Zairean Mass; the invocation of the ancestors is an entirely new element. Then we note the position of the penitential rite: while the Roman Mass has it in the introductory part (before the Gloria), the Zairean Mass uses it to conclude the liturgy of the Word. Another difference occurs with the greeting of peace. While the Roman Mass has it in the liturgy of the Eucharist as preparation for communion, the Zairean Mass has it in the liturgy of the Word as part of the penitential rite. The place of the invocation of the saints and ancestors, the penitential rite, and the greeting of peace is explained on cultural grounds.

The Invocation of the Ancestors

First, with regard to the invocation of saints and ancestors, both liturgical and anthropological considerations played important roles. The invocation, which usually takes the form of a litany, comes at the beginning of the Mass. According to the General Introduction to the approved text of the Mass of 1988, the assembly recognizes itself as poor before God and therefore calls on God's intimate friends, the saints and ancestors, to intercede on its behalf.

> In order to approach the Eucharist, the sacred action par excellence, the assembly recognizes its poverty in the presence of the Almighty God, the source of salvation. From the beginning of the sacred action, the living members invoke the saints, friends of God, as intercessors. The communion between the Christians on earth finds fulfillment in communion with the saints in heaven. It is in this that union with Christ (from whom flows the grace and the life of the people of God) is achieved. In the same way it is justified to invoke ancestors of sincere heart who are, in virtue of the merits of Christ, in communion with God, just as the Roman liturgy evokes from antiquity Abel the just, Abraham, and Melchizedek.[15]

This invocation of the saints and ancestors is made to establish a unity between the already triumphant church and the pilgrim church. It also seeks to obtain spiritual support for the living members who gather for worship. The invocation reveals the belief that the dead are not strangers to the present assembly of worship.

Africans have a strong attachment to their ancestors. Ancestors are seen as the means through whom the Creator God has transmitted life to the present generation. As noted in various studies of African rituals and the African sense of the sacred, celebrations usually begin with "rites of contact," which express the sense of the worshipers' littleness in the presence of the transcendent God. This feeling of littleness leads the worshipers to seek contact with their ancestors to act as intermediaries between them and God. Such rites also initiate the first act of communication between the worshiper and the worshiped.

Most tribes of black Africa would not begin a public ceremony without invoking the ancestors, who are believed to exercise real control over the living and under whose surveillance people live. By opening the celebration with the invocation of saints and ancestors, the Zairean Mass identifies the Christian assembly as the meeting place between the Creator, the ancestors, and the living. Placed at the beginning of the celebration, this invocation is not only an invitation to participate in the communion of saints. It is also an affirmation of the eschatological character of the Christian assembly as the memory of the already victorious church calls the attention of the pilgrim church to the reality of that heavenly Jerusalem "where Christ sits at God's right hand in his capacity as the eternal minister of the sanctuary and the tabernacle" (Vatican II, Constitution on the Sacred Liturgy, no. 8). The first movement in this liturgy is the establishment of contact and communion that established a sense of ease and communication in the life of the worshipers. This communion between the visible and the invisible is what evokes the outburst of praise in the Gloria.

Invoking the names of Mary the Mother of Christ, the patron saints of the parish church, the patron saints of all those present, and other saints is not new in Christian liturgy. The eucharistic prayers of the Roman rite have such invocations. What is new is the place in the liturgy at which this invocation is made as well as the fact that the ancestors are asked to become part of a celebration in which many of them never shared in their lifetimes.

What kind of saints are these ancestors? Do they correspond to what the church believes about saints? As the text reminds us, the memories of Old Testament figures like Abel, Abraham, and Melchizedek are used in the Roman liturgy. These persons, even though they are remembered in the Roman Mass, did not themselves share in the experience of the Christian Eucharist. The justification is made explicit in the words of invitation of the priest to the people before the invocation is made:

> Let us unite ourselves with all the disciples of Christ
> who have left this earth,
> and are now resting from their tiredness
> at God's side.
> Let us unite ourselves with all who,
> even though they had not known Christ in their lifetime,
> have however sought God with a sincere heart.
> With his [God's] help,
> they have accomplished his will,
> and are now with him.[16]

It is also important here to appreciate the African notion of the true ancestor. Not all the dead are ancestors. Moral excellence, bravery, successful social and family life, and other qualities are important criteria in establishing who is truly an ancestor. In some tribes it is still true that people who do not have offspring may never be regarded as ancestors, since they have no descendants to perpetuate their names. In some ways it is easier to become a Christian saint than it is to become an African ancestor. Calling on these ancestors evokes a good memory on the part of the worshipers who can think of a forefather or foremother whose life is worth emulating. If there is anything missing here in the Zairean text, it is the absence of

names of ancestors; while names of Christian saints are mentioned in the Roman eucharistic prayer, no names of ancestors
are indicated in the Zairean Mass.

The memory of these ancestors is re-echoed at the end of
the Preface. Each time the memory of the Christian saints
is evoked, that of the ancestors naturally follows, in a way
that the official commentary considers comparable to the
remembrances of the Old Testament personages.

The notion of the ancestor has continued to occasion de-
bate in theological and liturgical circles. Since Vatican II the
church has come to appreciate more the saving acts of God
that transcend geographic, racial, and religious boundaries.
This direct reference to African ancestors is one of the key
contributions of African theology to the emerging liturgical
rites on the African continent.

The Penitential Rite

Whereas the Roman Mass presents the rite of purification
(penitential rite) as the initial act of worship, the Zairean Mass
rather portrays the need for communion between the human
and the divine as the first movement in worship. For the Zairean Mass, the sense of sinfulness and the need for purification
belong to a later moment in the ritual. According to the official
commentary, the proclamation of the Word of God, followed
by the homily and the Creed, then evokes a triple response
from the people: the penitential rite, the greeting of peace, and
the "universal prayer." The first of these is the penitential rite.

The Word of God proclaimed in the assembly is effica-
cious and liberating: it makes a demand on the community, builds up the trust of the people of God, and
purifies their hearts. This purification is expressed in

the penitential rite whose structure has been inspired by African ritual and dialogical forms.[17]

The placing of the penitential rite here is seen as a sign of conversion following the announcement of the Word of God. The rationale for this placement is expressed in one of the documents of the Zairean bishops conference:

> The penitential act is placed after the liturgy of the Word in order to bring out the fact that it is the Word of God that reveals to us that we are sinners. It is also this Word that arouses in us the motivation for our conversion.[18]

Whereas the Roman Mass begins with the penitential rite, the Zairean Mass has the people enter the assembly with great rejoicing, only to recognize their failings after the Lord speaks.

Several African theologians and bishops have offered reasons to support the position of the penitential rite in the Zairean Mass. Speaking in Rome on the occasion of the Extraordinary Synod of Bishops, Bishop Anselme Sanon of Bobo-Dioulasso, Burkina-Faso, made the following remarks:

> Take the celebration of the Eucharist, for example. You begin it with a penitential liturgy. This is an approach that is altogether contrary to our own mentality. For we have the custom of first of all greeting one another before anything else, and then listening to the message that is brought to us.... Therefore, according to our own custom, the Word of God and the homily precede the confession of sins, contrary to what is customary.[19]

Taking a further step in support of this position, Elochukwu Uzukwu proposed a format for an Igbo Mass in Nigeria in which he placed the penitential rite after a community expression of commitment to God's Word following the homily.

This position of the penitential rite corresponds well to this section of the liturgy, where worshipers are becoming more conscious of what is involved in their relationship to God. It also corresponds well to the rhythm of traditional African rituals in which the rites of purification are performed only after certain preparatory rituals have taken place. Removing this ritual from the introductory part and putting it close to the center of the celebration helps to give it greater importance and prominence. In both the Roman and the Zairean Masses, the sprinkling of holy water on the people is part of the penitential rite. When this practice is performed at the beginning of the Mass, as in the Roman rite, the baptismal theme is predominant as the people gather as a community of the baptized. In the Zairean rite, the sprinkling also offers a form of "purification," which is a "reminder of baptism."

The change in position also has some ecumenical benefits, since a similar change had already occurred in the new Anglican liturgy.

The Greeting of Peace

After the penitential rite there follows the second response to the Word: the sharing of peace. This is different from the present Roman practice. Although the ancient tradition found in the Didache places the kiss after the penitential rite, that occurred when the penitential rite was at the beginning of the Mass. There is also another ancient tradition that placed the kiss of peace right after the prayer of the faithful. In the Zairean Mass, however, it precedes the prayer of the faithful.

By placing the kiss here the Zairean Mass associates it with the penitential rite. The kiss becomes an outward manifestation of inward conversion and reconciliation. Now that broken friendship has been mended in Christ, an expression of renewed friendship is appropriate. The sign of peace is therefore "the conclusion of the ritual of reconciliation."

The rite of peace manifests the peace recovered and its reinforcement among the people, as well as the harmony between God and the people. It is celebrated as the conclusion of the ritual of reconciliation, before the offering of the Eucharistic sacrifice, according to the Word of the Lord: "Go first and reconcile with your brother, and then come to make your offering" (Matt. 5:24). The sharing of peace completes the act of reconciliation.

The greeting of peace is performed in diverse ways depending on the region: washing hands in the same bowl and then making the sign of the cross, shaking the hands of the brothers and sisters in the assembly, an embrace.

The third and final response to the Word is the "universal prayer." After the sign of peace, the universal prayer signifies the fraternity of the believers and their need to have the world filled with peace. During these prayers, incense is burned where it accords with custom.

Ceremonial Differences

Apart from the structural differences, there are some ceremonial differences between the Roman and Zairean rites worth noting. We have already mentioned the announcer, whose role tends to be catechetical and helps to punctuate the celebration. Depending on the talents and abilities of the announcer, the level of the participation of the assembly in the liturgy can be very high, even when the presider does not inspire the people or move them to active participation. The announcer can become the community catalyst, firing up the assembly and raising the level of liturgical action.

During the liturgy of the Word, the lectors approach the presider for blessing before proclaiming the Word of God. The text indicates:

Before each reading, the lector goes and bows in front of the priest who is seated on his chair and asks his blessing. Whoever takes the word in the assembly in the name of the Holy God cannot proclaim it without the recognition of him who presides in the name of Christ. When he/she has received the blessing, the lector makes a sign of gratitude.

In the Roman rite, the deacon asks for a blessing from the presider before proclaiming the gospel. Why does the Zairean rite extend this practice to lectors?

One explanation flows from the nature of the role of the presider who is seen as a village chief. No one in the village assembly would rise to speak without first seeking the authority of the chief. The act of "giving the word" to someone is the sole way the power of speech is delegated to individual members of the village assembly.

This practice fortifies the position of the presider as the one who leads the ritual process, in the name of Christ. It may be argued that this practice reinforces clericalism and diminishes the baptismal right to proclaim the Word. There is, however, another interpretation of this practice. After all, no one is really worthy enough to serve in God's place, that is, to speak for God as such. We are made worthy only through adoption and grace. In asking and receiving the blessing, the lector is not really asking for permission to speak but rather to be able to minister effectively to the assembly through the outpouring of the grace of the Spirit.

There are other important elements that give the Zairean Mass its uniqueness. There is some difference in the ceremony of the presentation of gifts. The procession in song and dance and the words used during the presentation of the gifts bear marks of originality. Note that the words of the presentation are proclaimed by the entire assembly, rather than by the priest alone. Moreover, the gifts are truly from the people. What is not obvious in the approved text is the possibility that the people themselves might bake the bread and ferment the wine – a practice that is allowed but seldom carried out. When the liturgy speaks of "fruits of the earth and work of human hands," the earth refers to the Zairean soil, and the human hands are those of the people that assemble to worship. The Zairean church had not as yet pursued the question of local sacramental elements for the Eucharist.

The eucharistic prayer, although it is derived from Eucharistic Prayer II of the Roman Sacramentary, bears marks of both a native touch and distinctive theological positions.

* * * * *

To summarize, there are four areas in which the Zairean Mass demonstrates some structural independence from the Roman rite: the position of the invocation of saints, the inclusion of an invocation of ancestors, the position of the penitential rite, and the position of the kiss of peace. Other signs of its independence are the more powerful role of the presider, the role of the announcer, the more elaborate processions with dances (including the dances around the altar), the use of a distinctive eucharistic prayer, the music and song, the ceremony of the presentation of gifts, and the use of native costumes and instruments.

Structural Deficiencies of the Zairean Mass

The liturgy of the Word in the Zairean Mass is very congested and unduly heavy, compared to what one would expect in a typical Christian African celebration. For an assembly attuned to song, music, and dance, the prolongation of the liturgy of the Word is a tacit denial of basic characteristics of the people.

Why, for example, is it necessary to have three readings? A single proclamation of the Word would be sufficient.

The retention of the Gloria and the Credo in the liturgy is also evidence of an error of perspective. The Gloria repeats the action of the joyous entry in song and dance. It disrupts the natural flow of the celebration. The Credo duplicates the profession of faith expressed through the gathering of the assembly in the name of the Trinity. The structure and quality of the first part of the Mass would be better organized by removing the Gloria and the Credo. The first part of the liturgy would then be limited to: entrance in song and dance, invocation of ancestors in the faith, gathering prayer, reading, homily, penitential rite, kiss of peace, and prayer of the faithful, with some interlacing of invocations, greetings, songs, and movement.

The structure of the liturgy of the Eucharist in the Roman Missal has not been changed in the composition of the Zairean liturgy, with the exception of moving the kiss of peace to its earlier place in the Mass. Evidently responding attentively to official Roman positions, the commission has adhered to the spirit of the Roman Missal.

The Zairean Mass, by taking Eucharistic Prayer II of the Roman Missal and attaching some elements of African life and communication styles to it, has not given birth to an African eucharistic prayer. The internal structure, the content, and the general orientation of the Roman prayer do not suddenly become African simply by being sung with local rhythms. Wood, no matter how long it stays in the river, can never become a crocodile. It is curious why the Zairean commission was not inspired by the numerous efforts and noted successes made in the composition of African eucharistic prayers. As early as 1970 such efforts had already yielded several eucharistic prayers that were being seriously considered for use in many African dioceses.

The communion and the dismissal rites in the Zairean liturgy have nothing new or remarkable in them, except for the recession in music, song, and dance.

Ministers and Ministry

Let us now look more closely at the specific roles played in this celebration. We will also touch again on major aspects of the celebration itself, bearing in mind those elements that help to identify the Zairean liturgy as a distinctive experience of celebration.

The Presider

The presider in this celebration is fully in charge of the worship of the assembly. He is seen as "one who presides in the name of Christ." He mirrors the role of the traditional African chief, whose position and role in traditional African life is extremely important. In Uganda for example, the king of Buganda was seen as the sum and substance of the whole community. The entire people were supposed to be personified in their king. He was the living father of all the people, upon whom all filial love, respect, and obedience were focused. All things belonged to him; the land and all its properties were under his patronage. Authorities in the families, villages, counties, and throughout the land were considered to have originated from him, whom they regarded as "father" of all.

When the "Ooni of Ife," who is a powerful traditional ruler among the Yoruba people of western Nigeria, emerges from his palace on a festive day, all the musicians, drummers, singers, and dancers of the village make music to praise him, while the elders and palace councilors pay him homage. A mere lifting of his fan or staff of office will immediately bring everyone to complete silence. The Ooni is the political, ritual, and legal ruler. At times, the national president of the country has less power in a given region than the local chief.

There are also women in chieftaincy positions and local ritual leadership who would command similar respect when they minister in those capacities. There are priestesses in charge of shrines in Yorubaland; across Africa, women have healing ministries; and women are custodians of birth places. The Zairean liturgy, however, does not discuss or introduce any hints about whether a woman could preside over a eucharistic celebration.

In the Zairean Mass, the presider's use of the horse tail and the goatskin hat as well as his being surrounded by acolytes swinging spears portrays royalty and power. The presider delegates the power of speech in the assembly, most evident in the case of the lectors who must ask and receive his blessing before proclaiming the Word:

> May the Lord help you
> so that your eyes may be illumined;
> may the words that your mouth proclaims
> bring consolation to the hearts of men.[20]

His role as the mediator between God and the people is seen in the words used by the gift-bearers when they present the gifts to him at the offering:

> O Priest of God,
> here are our gifts.
> Receive them.

It should be noted that in the approved text, the use of the term "ministers" does not include the presiding priest and the priest-concelebrants. These are consistently referred to as "priests" and are distinguished from other "ministers." For example, in describing one of the functions of the announcer, it says:

Before the Mass begins, the announcer introduces the priest or priests, the ministers, and eventually the notable visitors who have come to associate with the community.

In other words, when the approved text uses the term "ministers," it is referring to those without Orders (the announcer, the lectors, etc.). This narrow definition of ministry in the eucharistic celebration leads to some unwarranted conclusions.

Because this distinction is consistent, the approved text tacitly denies the priests full participation in the dance during the celebration, whether during the processions or around the altar. Even when the priest is included, the use of the word "may" waters down the strength of the liturgical importance of dance. Unfortunately, this text avoids the use of the word "dance." Compare it, for example, with the rubric of an earlier 1980 text that includes the priest in the dancing:

Recognizing that the assembly of all those united in Christ is a sign of the presence of the kingdom, the people sing a song of glory and praise to God. The presider (or another minister) now adds some more incense to the fire. Depending on the liturgical time, the Gloria or any other appropriate song may be sung. The people dance to the rhythm of the song from their places, while the presider and all the ministers dance around the altar.

This move to bracket out the priests from the rest of the assembly with regard to dancing during the liturgy is not Zairean but Roman. The Roman liturgy continuously isolates the priest from the assembly. African ritual leaders, while playing special roles at worship, ordinarily join fully in the action of worship of the assembly. In the eucharistic assembly of African people the priest-presider is also minister and dancer. In spite of the attempt of the approved text to isolate the priest from the rest of the assembly, however, in the actual celebration of the Zairean Mass the priest does in fact participate in the music, song, and dance.

The Announcer

The announcer plays a strategic role in the celebration. At the beginning of the celebration and at several peak moments, he or she calls people's attention to some message or some event. This minister announces the commencement of the celebration, introduces the readings and the proclamation of the eucharistic prayer. He or she introduces the priests and other ministers at the beginning of the Mass and, later, any special guests at the celebration. The announcer "provides the liaison between the priest and the assembly," and "very carefully inspires the active participation of the faithful in the celebration and through the prayers." According to the approved text, the announcer should not use improvised words during his or her interventions, but rather should use prepared written texts that bear witness to the mystery of Word and Sacrament as celebrated in the liturgy. It is the announcer's voice that is heard first in the celebration. The instrument of office for the announcer is the bell or gong. The sounding of the instrument is a formal call of all the people to attention. It is an indication that important information concerning the mystery of the celebration is about to be delivered.

Sometimes the sound of the instrument itself is the message. Those who perform such a ministry must be trained to make a given sound with the instrument, since particular sounds signify particular messages to the people. A typical example can be illustrated from this testimony of a missionary in Zaire, who tells of the use of a wooden musical instrument called the *tshionda*.

I see it as part of my missionary life to preserve everything genuinely cultural. We first tried to find an authentic "tshionda" (hollow tree with opening on the upper
side). One of our male nurses found one and learned
to use it as a drum. Once he had mastered the skill,
he went to an old farmer to learn the different beats
for joyful events, for mourning, for war and for peace.
From the many "melodies" he brought, we selected a
few that now serve to make our liturgy more indigenous
and more real for the thousands of simple people who
come from all the hamlets in the neighborhoods. We now
use the tshionda to announce the coming of Christ the
King on Palm Sunday just as the Chief would have been
announced in the past. On Good Friday, the news of
Christ's death is communicated in the same way that in
yesteryear, the news of the death of a Chief was spread
through the villages.[21]

The use of sound instruments as communication tools is
common in Zaire.

The ministry of the announcer is parallel to that of the
town crier in a typical African village. The town crier is usually someone with a very good and clear voice. Walking or
riding around the village and striking his or her instrument,
the town crier delivers a consistent message to the people.
A village head wishing to convoke an emergency meeting of
the elders or all the people, would send out the information
through the town crier, who carries out the responsibility very
late at night or before cock-crow in the morning. At this time,
people are expected to be home, and in the quiet environment
of the village, the message is brought to waking ears.

There is no doubt that the ministry of the announcer was
inspired by that of the town crier. Walking down the aisle,
striking the gong, and calling the people's attention to the fact

that the liturgy is about to begin reminds the people that the event deserves their respect. There is also a similarity between this ministry and that of the village catechist, who formerly introduced the different parts of the Mass to the people in their local languages – at a time when everything else was said in Latin. The announcer's role in speaking at certain moments accentuates important parts of the celebration.

The Deacon

The Zairean Mass did not initially include any role for the deacon. The Zairean church had already developed a very effective ministry of the *mokambi*. These ministers, men and women alike, were very active in the spiritual and ritual leadership of the local churches. They were trained catechists who sometimes served as pastors in rural areas where priests visited only rarely. These *mokambi* had more important liturgical roles than the traditional deacon. But their ministry did not fit into any of the categories in the official books of the Roman church. Therefore, as a result of the demand made by Roman authorities that the role of the deacon in the Zairean Mass be specified, the liturgical commission determined the following: the deacon carries the book of the gospels, proclaims the gospel, helps the priest to receive the gifts brought by the people at the offering, helps the priest at the altar, and says or sings the closing words: "Go, in the peace of Christ." The *mokambi* thus do not have official roles in this celebration. In practice, however, they are pastoral leaders in communities without priests.

The Lector

According to Father Mpoto M. L. Mpongo, who served as the diocesan spokesperson, there is a "revalorization of the ministry of lector" in this celebration. If the liturgical laws of the church were consistent, there would have been an insistence that only those commissioned or instituted as lectors would be allowed to proclaim the Word in public worship.[22] In the Zairean Mass, the non-commissioned lector who approaches the presider to ask for and receive a blessing is by that fact receiving the church's mandate to minister to the community in that liturgy. Only in that way, he argues, would such a person stand to speak to the assembly in the name of God.

The Zairean liturgy allows women as well as men to proclaim the Word as lectors. The French text regularly says: "le lecteur ou la lectrice." This provision differs from the Roman practice, which ordinarily institutes only men as lectors. (Of course in liturgical practice, women minister as lectors in dioceses around the world.)

Gestures in the Liturgy

The presider's initial veneration of the altar is done with a deep bow, a genuflection, a prostration, or a kiss of the four sides of the altar. The assembly stands from the entrance procession to the opening prayer, during the enthronement of the gospel, during the Creed, during the penitential rite and the peace, from the eucharistic prayer to the beginning of communion, for the communion prayer, and for the final blessing and sending forth. They sit during the readings, including the gospel, a practice taken from native experience in which the chief delivers important messages before a seated audience. People who are standing seem to be in a hurry to leave, although a standing position is, of course, necessary during liturgical dance, processions, etc. The Good News, argues one pastor in Kinshasa, must be proclaimed before willing, respecting, and patient ears. For this reason, sitting during the gospel – as during any other proclamation of the Word in the assembly – is preferable to standing. The people sit also during the bringing of the gifts and the distribution of communion. The people raise their hands before and during the prayers said by the priest (opening, offertory, and communion) during the doxology, and during the Our Father.

During the penitential rite, they manifest an attitude of sorrow, for example, holding down the head and crossing the hands on the breast. Such gestures of humility and guilt are important improvements over the ambiguous Roman symbol of striking the breast thrice. In parts of Africa, striking the breast suggests defiance.

During the eucharistic prayer, they may remain standing or kneel, according to local requirement. If they kneel, they rise before the doxology.

The outward manifestation of a "sign of gratitude" at certain moments of the celebration is another mark of the Zairean Mass. When the lectors receive the blessings from the priest before their proclamations, they thank him in a visible way; when the priest delivers the homily, they clap for him in gratitude; when the priest receives the gifts from the people, he thanks them by clapping, and the people clap because they are happy that the priest has received their offering for God.

The Zairean Mass encourages full participation of the people at different levels: through acclamations, gestures, singing, dancing, responses, music, clapping, rhythmic movements, shouts of joy, processions, and dialogical preaching. The whole community raising up its hands during the presidential prayers, the bowing and crossing of arms on the breast during the penitential rite, clapping and moving rhythmically to the flow of songs and music, crying out amid the sounds of musical instruments at peak moments of the celebration

(such as during the processions and the consecration), dancing in the processions, singing the explosive "Glory to God in
the highest" and "Holy, Holy, Holy" accompanied by dances
around the altar — all these give the Zairean Mass its local
identity.

Chapter 4

African
Values and Symbols
in the Zaïrean Mass

Values and beliefs are alive and relevant when they are celebrated in rites by living women and men. Rites give flesh and authenticity to beliefs and values. Here we will assess how African values are reflected in the liturgy, the concrete ways in which the people's life, beliefs, and needs are expressed in the new rite and, in some cases, how they could be better expressed.

God of All Creation

Africentric worship, of course, concerns the people's response to the activity and revelations of the Creator God. Peoples of African descent are well known for their unparalleled attachment to God and to all things religious. Life itself is religion. Any reference to life among African peoples is inevitably a reference to the activity of God in the community. The place of God in the life of the people is central and unchallenged.

This God is truly alive and active, kind and forgiving, strong and glorious, creative and protective, and lives in everlasting communion with all.

When the community sings, dances, makes music, listens, prays or proclaims the word, it is all in testimony of the wonders of God among the people. These wonders include the joys and the pains, the hopes and the anxieties of the entire community. African people profess that God is part of everyday experience, whether beautiful or ugly. It is with that attachment to God that ugly moments are bearable. That is why the liturgical assembly is the place for everyone to come: to cry out their pain and sing out their joy.

In the text and celebration of the Zairean liturgy, God has the uppermost hand in the celebration. God is the reason for the gathering, the invocations, the prayers, the proclamations, the dance, the music, the reconciliation, the presentations and offerings, the praise and worship, the dedication, the remembering, the sharing, the thanksgiving, the blessing, and the apostolic commission to the world. This is a basic assumption necessary for understanding the entire text and celebration.

Of course, Europeans and Americans who have been very busy debating the problem of liturgical language and the genderization of the image of God in worship will find the text of the Zairean liturgy insensitive to these issues. God in the Zairean liturgy is masculine. Missionary Christianity preached God so. We should also note the French influence on Africa. Zaire was colonized by French-speaking Belgium. In the French language, a large group of women (feminine) suddenly becomes grammatically masculine simply by the introduction of a baby boy into the group. The people of Zaire do not find it unusual to describe God as a masculine figure. In traditional African life, however, God is presented in both feminine and masculine images. Since this topic is also a theological issue confronting the church today, it is important that liturgists be sensitive to it.

Family and Community

African people are family-oriented, and Zaireans are no exception. Of course, fathers and mothers, brothers and sisters come together in this eucharistic worship. Indeed the entire extended family shares in the worship of the assembly, including a large number of young people.

Living men and women gather in union with the saints and ancestors, as one family, to worship God. The family is so extended and elastic that it transcends time and place. At the invitation to the invocation of saints and ancestors, the presider says:

> With all those who sleep in peace,
> we form one single family.
> May this eucharistic sacrifice
> gather all of us into one single family before God.[23]

This theme is further expressed when the gifts for the offering are presented as manifesting "our spirit of solidarity and sharing, and the fact that we love one another as the Lord has loved us." It is this spirit of solidarity that makes the sense of celebration so real in the Zairean liturgy.

The sense of community is exhibited in the "we" texts that mark the prayers of the liturgy. The priest who leads the assembly in the penitential rite of the Mass prays:

> Before the Virgin Mary,
> before all the saints,
> before our brothers and sisters
> we recognize that our hearts have been far from you.

We have honored you only with our lips.
Lord have mercy.[24]

The "we" of the Zairean liturgy is geographically limited in scope. One would expect that in the current environment of intertribal conflicts, family ruptures, betrayal of friendships and trust, and other acts of hatred and sin that disturb the community, a truly African liturgy would celebrate concrete acts of repentance and reconciliation. The penitential rite is a suitable place to celebrate renewal of friendships, family reconciliations, and rituals of recommitment of public officials to the public good.

When the people sing and dance, they do so as a community. Together they swing to the left and to the right; they clap according to the rhythm of the song. Gestures are done in unison, and they add melody to form a beautiful result.

Nonetheless, the Zairean Mass does not reflect the reality of the tribal conflicts and discord that continue to destroy human community in Zaire and across the African continent. The liturgy lacks an emphasis on the need for real unity, reconciliation, and peace among the peoples and the tribes. It has left a very sensitive issue of contemporary African life unattended.

Traditionally, Africans who do not commune or communicate — due to quarrels, for example — do not celebrate together without first being reconciled. Traditional reconciliation could be done through a blood pact, an oath, or a symbolic or ritual sharing of food or drink. Village, family, or ritual heads regularly preside over such acts of reconciliation, for example, between husband and wife, between wives of a polygamist, or between landowners. This kind of ministry cries out for expression in Christian communities around the African continent where public enemies participate in the liturgies, share in the sacramental bread and cup, and then go away to continue their mutual acts of mischief and hatred. Such scandal violates the spirit of the eucharistic liturgy.

Justice, Peace, and Human Promotion

African cultures that elevate the family, the community, and human life in general require people to be sensitive to the needs of others, especially the underprivileged, to assure harmony and progress in the extended family. Awareness of the plight of the poor of the community has been demonstrated in some texts of the Zairean liturgy. In the opening rubric of the 1980 edition of the liturgy, it states:

> The people arrive from their various homes and exchange greetings. Each one normally brings something for the offering. In fact, "it is proper for the faithful to show their participation by bringing either the bread or the wine for the celebration of the Eucharist, or other gifts that will be used to sustain the Church and its needy members (*Ordo Missae*, n. 13)."

Unfortunately, this recommendation seems to represent more of an academic position than real practice. Some who have worshiped at the celebration of the Zairean Mass have been quick to comment on the possibility of the liturgy becoming an opium for the people in the face of the serious hardships they go through all their lives.

This question has been addressed by Zairean liturgists. Some do not think that the liturgy leaves the issue totally unattended. According to them, there are two levels of approach to the issue. First, the Zairean liturgy, in the spirit of 1 Peter 2:13, prepares the assembly for good conduct in the world. They cite the penitential prayer in the Mass, which says:

Before you, Lord Jesus,
we recognize that
if the world does not know you,
if there are injustices,
if there is hatred and enmity,
it is because we are not true witnesses of your kingdom.
O Christ have mercy.

Second, they argue that although there are the didactic aspects of the liturgy, it is catechetics that needs to bring issues of justice more into focus. Liturgy and catechetics must work together in this regard, they maintain.

The penitential rite in this Mass does, of course, imply an effort to lead a good life. It also asks for sincere conversion and reconciliation, and these are important for the goals of human promotion. Even the sign of peace shared immediately after the penitential rite reinforces this need for good interpersonal relationships. The sharing of the peace in Christ has a social implication too. However, we insist that an authentic African liturgy today should not stop at preaching justice; it should do justice. Within the context of that celebration, concrete acts of commitment on the part of the assembly are important to give flesh to the good news of Christ. The social conditions that the ordinary people of Zaire live in call for immediate reaction. The close relationship between liturgy (and especially the eucharistic liturgy) and social justice in early Christian practice (see, e.g., Acts 2:42-47) reminds us that the church's most important act of worship carries with it the obligation of truly caring for the welfare of Christ's body here and now.

The relationship between liturgy and social justice continued to elude the theologians directly involved with shaping the Zairean Mass. It is surprising that they were not inspired by the high volume of statements coming from the Holy See and numerous African church leaders on justice, peace, and human promotion issues. Liturgical practice in Africa has not really been emancipated from the monopoly of the spiritual domain, a hang-up inherited from missionary Christianity, which separated body and spirit in the act of worship.

Why has the Zairean liturgy not adopted the kind of strong language that African bishops have to challenge oppressive leaders and demand for peace and reconciliation? Why has it been difficult for this liturgy to embody love toward the hungry and the naked of the community? Why couldn't the people bring food at the time of the offerings and give it to the needy of the community after communion? Why not initiate actions to seek shelter for the homeless who sing and clap at the liturgy only to return to homelessness afterward?

Besides, if the Zairean liturgy is acting as standard bearer for the African churches, why is international peace not spoken about? What about tribal conflicts raging in Uganda and Burundi, for example? Why was the rite not concerned about apartheid in South Africa when it was the world's most outrageous evil? Is it not curious that these sad experiences of other Africans go unmentioned even in the prayer of the faithful in the Zairean celebrations? Perhaps the people have not been made aware enough of the evils of society around them. Perhaps catechesis has not included the social dimensions of liturgical experience.

The issue of liberation in Africa certainly goes beyond the political, religious, and cultural arenas and touches other areas of experience, including the economic. The evolution of authentic African liturgies must include a growing sensitivity to the socio-economic experiences of the communities. There is no continent today more harassed by human injustice, hunger, drought, alienation, disease, and death than Africa. Liturgies termed "African" that neglect these aspects of the people's lives will continue to be alien, no matter who puts them together. If an African liturgy is conceived as one in which the people, after leaving their leaking roofs, gather with empty stomachs for a period of two hours, clap, sing, and dance, and then return to their previous situations of want and abject poverty, those in charge of such a liturgy must be ready in the long run to do it without the people. "A hungry stomach does not listen to the Word of God" according to a well-known African saying – and certainly not for a long time! In a culture that prides itself on its "African humanism," it does not make any sense to see monumental and very expensive church buildings being erected with pennies extracted from undernourished poor people.

The Zairean Mass has little place for the direct care of the many people who come to it with such high expectations for their human survival; this is a tragic omission.

Recently, an archdiocesan synod at Kinshasa stated that the desire expressed on all sides to continue the effort of creativity and inculturation manifests the profound need to relate the liturgy to life. The liturgical experience of the people should assist in finding the strength for a daily commitment to justice and truth.

Hospitality

In the Zairean liturgy, members of the assembly as well as visitors are usually welcomed with open arms. In order to provide visitors a good opportunity to see what happens in the sanctuary space and at the same time to help them feel part of the movement in the assembly, the Parish of St. Alphonse at Kinshasa-Matete has special seating for guests and visitors in the middle of the assembly. The most inhibited visitors who arrive in church wondering and looking, with hands in their pockets, often end up clapping and dancing and singing, even without knowing the words to the songs. After the thanksgiving song and dance following communion, visitors are welcomed by an acclamation of the community.

There is, however, an aspect of African hospitality that poses a problem for Catholic liturgy in Africa. Full participation in the reception of holy communion is reserved to a select group of Catholic faithful. African hospitality requires that those who have a place at the ritual have a right to share in its meals. This aspect of African spirituality could help to redefine the meaning of "worthiness" and "unworthiness" with regard to participating in the eucharistic elements. In other words, all Catholics who participate in the celebration should participate in the meal, not because they have been found worthy on their own merits, but because they are being made worthy by the blood of the lamb. The Eucharist after all is for the healing of those who yearn for the saving hand of God in Christ.

This is also the place to raise the question of allowing non-Catholic Christians to participate in communion if they have participated in the Mass. And there is also the question of non-Christians who join in the Sunday liturgies (as often happens) and expect to be invited for communion. In traditional African religion, one may be refused ritual participation for several reasons; for example: ritual impurity, social violations, or public scandals. If exclusion is not made in the first place, it should not be done at the meal. The Zairean Mass does not show sensitivity to this aspect of African hospitality.

There are other practices inconsistent with African hospitality. Giving people consecrated bread reserved for days in the tabernacle (though not favored by the church but regularly done) is questionable by African standards. Although not recommended by the text, communion is often distributed at the celebration from reserves. African people do not usually serve leftover food at feasts. In many instances, the goat or the cow to be eaten is slaughtered before everyone as part of the ritual. Then as many as possible participate in the ritual of the preparation of the meal.

Life, Wholeness, and Healing

The text glides quickly over the subject of human life. Although life in general is implied in the creation references and the celebration of human presence at the assembly, there is not a clear articulation of the centrality of human life in the spirituality of the people. This subdued reference to life ultimately affects the way the themes of wholeness and healing are handled in this celebration.

The liturgy explicitly mentions healing on two occasions in the preparatory prayers for the reception of holy communion, just as they appear in the Roman Mass. First, it is mentioned in the alternative prayer of the presider just before communion:

> Lord Jesus Christ,
> we shall share your body and blood.
> May this communion bring us
> neither judgment nor condemnation.
> Instead, let it uphold us,
> and become the remedy that brings us healing.

Since this is the second of two alternative prayers, there is only the possibility of its being used in the liturgy. In other words, healing is not really the predominant theme here, but rather the deliverance from sin and evil that we find in the first of the alternative prayers. This predominant theme is also seen in the presider's invitation to the assembly to share in the Lord's meal: "Here is the Lamb of God who takes away the sins of the world." This is a clear case of Roman influence on this liturgy.

The response of the assembly to this invitation is the second mention of healing in the text.

> Lord, I am not worthy to receive you,
> but only say the word
> and I shall be healed.

The theology of the Eucharist exhibited in these prayers sees the Eucharist as able to procure the forgiveness of sins, offer some form of healing, and prepare one for eternal life. The sense of healing here does not go beyond what is generally implied in the Roman liturgy, expression of faith reflecting the profession of the centurion in the gospel. The Roman Mass does not develop the theme of healing beyond that of the spiritual liberation of the faithful from evil and sin.

The Zairean Mass has imitated this stunted vision of healing. What is lacking is a clear indication of the need for both corporal and spiritual healing of individual participants and the community, as well as an incorporation of some ritual of healing into the celebration. This is a serious omission on the part of the composers of the liturgy, especially because the ministry of healing occupies a strategic place in the worship experience of African peoples.

Healing is a much subdued theme in the theology of the Catholic theologians in Africa, and the Zairean Mass is correspondingly low-keyed on the subject. In response, the Indigenous African Christian Churches have claimed to be more reliable and authentic for Africans than the institutional missionary churches.

The Zairean liturgy could incorporate healing into the celebration. There could be a healing ritual during the penitential rite, especially in those cases where it is believed that the cause of the illness or malaise could be the wrongdoings of the individuals concerned. The prayer of the faithful could be an occasion to perform a rite of exorcism over the afflicted, with

anointing and the laying on of hands in prayer over the sick
of the community. The eucharistic prayer could incorporate
the themes of spiritual and physical healing of the community.
The sharing in the bread and wine should be done in a way
that expresses the sustaining of life and health in Christ. The
celebration could end with a prayer/blessing asking for peace
and the protection of the people from evil.

Women

The most prominent manifestation of the presence of women
in the celebration of the Zairean Mass is usually in the assembly space: women outnumber men by a wide margin. The
choir also includes a majority of women. Women serve as lectors, announcers, and gift-bearers. But the Zairean Mass leaves
no one in doubt about who presides at the celebration: the
male priest. Why are women stripped of their traditional role
as custodians of the nutritional elements in the community?
Since when have African men taken over every authority for
ritual sacrifices and meals? Similar questions are being asked
around the world in theological circles; the issues are anthropological as well as theological. The roles allowed to women
in this celebration – lector, cantor, announcer, and member of
the congregation – do not exhaust the possibilities envisioned
by an African understanding of the role of women in an adult
worshiping community.

The question of genderization here is acute. Even though
some effort has been made to incorporate women into the celebration at various levels, especially during the first half of the
Mass, they suddenly become recipients from the moment of
the eucharistic prayer to the end. It is curious that women are
not the ones who "prepare" the meal on the altar and share it
among the assembly, a task that rightfully belongs to them in

traditional African life. The model of the male Zairean chief as presider in this celebration may have contributed to this problem. There is need to appropriate female images and symbols in the culture, as well as to integrate female roles from African models of celebration. With regard to ministry in the church, it should be remembered that since 1967 women in Zaire have been ministering as out-station pastors, regularly preaching the Sunday homily and presiding at communion services.

Ancestors

At the beginning of the liturgy, the presider leads the assembly in a litany that seeks to unite the pilgrim church with the already victorious church. In this context, the ancestors are invoked as co-sharers of the divine presence. The priest's invitation to the people says:

Let us unite ourselves to all the followers of Christ
who have left this world
and are resting from their tiredness in the presence of God.
Let us unite ourselves to those who,
even if they did not know Christ in their lifetime,
did however seek God with a sincere heart.
Aided by God himself, they did his will;
they too are with him.
Together with all those who sleep in peace,
we form one single family.
May this eucharistic sacrifice
gather all of us into one family before God.

In the litany that follows, after the names of Mary mother of Christ, the patriarchs, prophets, apostles, evangelists, and all the heavenly saints, "our ancestors of upright heart" are invoked. They are called those who, "aided by God, served him faithfully." They are here seen in the light of the Old Testament personages who did not know Christ but who had led a life inspired by God. They *ipso facto* share God's presence today.

The reference to Old Testament personages in this context poses two problems. First, it tends to push the ancestors into a very remote past. Even the inclusion of the name of Melchizedek introduces an air of mystery, since that figure has no known origins in the Old Testament (see Heb. 7:3). African ancestors on the other hand are neither remote nor mythical. Ancestors do not have to have passed away a very long time ago. Second, the Old Testament reference weakens the traditional argument that these ancestors are righteous in their own right, that is, by virtue of their lives and roles then and now. African ancestors do not seek authenticity through Old Testament personages.

The memory of the ancestors is also recalled during the eucharistic prayer, as the church prays for those who have died in the hope of resurrection or salvation: "those who have left this earth of whom you know their hearts, all those whom you love and who have loved you."

Having concluded that an African liturgy should incorporate the alliance of people with their ancestors, the composers of the prayers of the Zairean Mass nonetheless seem to have been satisfied with a simple mention of the world "ancestor" without any mention of names. A central African value is simply grafted on to Roman texts, thus missing the point of the incarnational project. Similarly, all the eucharistic prayers composed in middle-belt Africa since 1970 have made mention of the "ancestors," but unfortunately none has mentioned any names.

There are other deficiencies as well. First, with the exception of Mary the mother of Christ, this litany makes no mention of women. Even the generic words used to designate biblical figures do not include female personages such as, for example, matriarchs and prophetesses. Nor does the text indicate whether women can become ancestors.

Second, with the single exception of the name of Mary, in the final approved text of the Zairean Mass only generic titles (patriarchs, prophets, apostles, evangelists, saints, ancestors) are used in the litany. Earlier versions of the text mentioned names for some of the saints, for example, the patron saint of the parish church and the saint of the day. This was consistent with the practice in the Roman Mass in which names of saints are indicated when references are made to them. The generalized designations avoid the need to mention names of ancestors. This is simply a narrow solution to a blessed opportunity.

Ancestors are not mental concepts but historical people. Among the Yoruba of Nigeria, some have been divinized. Among the Igbo, their names surface in traditional rituals. If grounds exist for mentioning ancestors at all, then they should be mentioned by name. What must be avoided is the multiplication of names, like what occurred on the church's calendar in the Middle Ages. At the same time, there should be no attempt to generalize the veneration of ancestors in sub-Saharan Africa, for there are some groups, like the Nuer of Sudan, that do not practice ancestor cults.

Third, the text of the Zairean Mass attests to a poverty of words and expressions to refer to the ancestors. The text gives some indication of who the ancestors are, but it does not say anything about what their roles are in the life of the people. The underlying motive in the Zairean texts seems to be to explain to the outside world who the African ancestors are; Africans already know what kind of people their ancestors are. This falls short of explaining why ancestors are being invoked in this liturgy.

Traditionally, ancestors are seen as the source of the unity, survival, and life of their offspring; they regulate the moral order and act to render justice in the name of the Creator; they are custodians of law and order in the tribe. These notions are important in understanding why African theologians believe that no one can arbitrarily decide to break away from the tribe, which is organized under the guidance of the ancestors. These various functions of the ancestors ought to be part of the prayer texts that refer to them in any African liturgy. The litany that commemorates the ancestors could end with a prayer acknowledging their participation in the celebration. In view of African rituals of communion with ancestors it would be appropriate at communion time to offer a piece of the consecrated bread and some of the consecrated wine to the ancestors as in a libation.

Local Imagery

The prayers of the Zairean Mass resound with local images. The image of the great Zaire River comes alive in the prayer concluding the penitential rite, which metaphorically asks that "our sins be cleansed in the deep and silent water of your mercy." Twice in the celebration, God is called the "sun that we cannot fix our eyes upon," a reference that readily calls to mind the hot Zairean sun that burns all year round. In the Preface of the eucharistic prayer, we have a description of riches of the environment: life, sky, earth, rivers, ponds, lakes, fishes, stars, birds, forests, plains, savannahs, mountains, and animals. Expressive of the local experience is the reference to the "blood-sucker" in the penitential rite:

> Lord our God,
> as the blood-sucker sticks onto the skin
> and sucks human blood,
> evil has invaded us.
> Our life is weakened.

The Zairean Mass is still dependent, however, on the Roman Sacramentary for its opening prayer, prayer over the gifts, and prayer after communion, as well as in other texts and possible alternatives. Even the prayer of peace that concludes the sharing of peace in this Mass, in spite of its originality, is proposed as an *alternative* to that of the Roman Missal. The prayers of the Roman Sacramentary have been criticized by African theologians as being too dry and too sober, too short, and in general non-enriching for Africans who communicate by imagery, story, and symbols. This constitutes one of the liturgy's weaknesses at this time. The need to create prayers with a local, poetic character should be one of the next priorities of the Episcopal Conference in Zaire.

A greater effort should be made to evaluate not only the structures and style of traditional African prayers, but most especially their content. In these prayers the preoccupations of the people are manifested.

Local Sacramental Elements

The ritual of the presentation of gifts is a very important aspect of public worship in African life. In this liturgy the people themselves pronounce the words of the presentation. The gifts come from the people, and the people present them to God through the ministry of the presider. The presider's part is limited to receiving the gifts, demonstrating appreciation for them, and saying the prayer over them.

Two types of gifts are usually presented: first, bread and wine for the Eucharist and, second, other gifts — in practice, usually money collected from the people. Because Zaire is an agricultural country, it would be appropriate for the people to bring the produce of their land as gifts during the Eucharist. Even though the text of the Mass indicates this preference, it has not been encouraged in practice. Such gifts could be used to the benefit of the many unfed and less fortunate members of the assembly and beyond. There is a poverty of expression and lack of commitment in the words used for this first presentation ("O priest of God, here are our gifts. Receive them. They show our spirit of solidarity and sharing and that we love one another as the Lord has loved us"). An improvement of expression would inevitably follow a reorientation of purpose and a change in the type of gifts brought by the people.

With regard to the bread and wine of the Eucharist, the sense of people offering to God what God has given them is also diminished. By simply saying that the bread and wine come from the fields and from the work of human hands, this presentation accommodates the offering of elements that have been imported from elsewhere. The question is: which fields? If we are not talking about Zairean fields and Zairean hands, then it is difficult to see how this ritual can claim to be authentically Zairean. Earlier versions of the text recommended that people bring the bread and the wine in the spirit of the Roman Missal. This provision was suppressed in the final text.

The issue of the eucharistic elements was not really given much attention in the work of the liturgy commission in Zaire. Consequently, the bread and wine of the celebration have remained the imported wafers and wines. This, in my opinion, is one of the fundamental flaws in their work. Why did the commission not undertake a study of the food plants of Zaire in order to make some proposal in this regard? The banana and palm are rich in both religious and economic symbolism in the region. Together they also symbolize the complementarity of the sexes. Other Zairean food products like cassava, rice, and palm wine are also logically and theologically sound for sacramental use in the Zairean liturgy.

In the arguments against the use of local elements for the Eucharist, there is a certain uncritical attachment to tradition that is not open to the incarnational implications of Jesus the Christ. Karl Rahner raised questions concerning the incarnational exigencies of celebrating the Eucharist in parts of the world where the traditional eucharistic elements are unavailable or scarce. The God of Christianity does not go visiting and carry a pot of food along.

Other Local Products for Christian Worship

The use of local insignia and instruments in the Zairean Mass has yielded a mixed reaction. Participants at the celebration often make positive comments from the point of view of aesthetics. Local instruments add to the color of the processions, the sanctuary, and the entire celebration. However, commenting on some of the gestures and costumes used in the Zairean Mass — especially the presider's hat and horse tail and the spears borne by acolytes — some observer-theologians have wondered if this celebration is not simply some form of folklore, a portrayal of the past that does not use language and symbol better suited to the present day. Charles Vandame, archbishop of N'Djamena, Chad, once referred to the Zairean Mass as the "Latin rite with local changes in dress and song."[25]

More serious is the argument against these insignia from local Zairean liturgical commissions. The pastors and members of the liturgical commission of Mbandika, Zaire, made the following remarks concerning the carrying of lances and knives:

> Our people are saying that the bearing of arms is not suitable at the eucharistic celebration. All of our people say that this will always remind one of war, combat, power, and force. More so when this concerns the great Chief, *Nkumu*, in his official costume. In this case, the carrying of arms signifies not only his authority, but above all his

power which terrifies his enemies and even his subjects. Therefore the priest, another Christ, in his salvific ministry, the work of divine mercy, the work of reconciliation among men and women and God, cannot manifest his power or authority by the carrying of arms.

In short, they would argue, not everything that is beautiful is liturgically sound.

The use of African costumes in the Zairean Mass has to be seen in its general, ritual perspective. Aesthetics is very important in African worship experience, but that is not the only reason for the things used in African worship. Certain things are used because they serve as memorials, and a people without memory is a people without a future. To use the symbol of the cross, for example, is not to advocate crucifixion in our time; rather it is a memorial of the means of Christian salvation. Likewise, the spear used in the celebration of the Zairean Mass is not intended as sign of readiness for battle, but rather as a symbol of the means that led to the freedom and security of the people.

Power and authority are aspects of African kingship, and the presider in the celebration of the Zairean Mass has power and authority.

Oral Tradition

The Zairean liturgy manifests some sensitivity to the oral character of traditional African life. This is evident in the prayer forms (with their short, repetitive lines), gestures, songs, dance, responses, dependence on memory, and some openness to creative spontaneity.

According to the document used to introduce the Zairean liturgy, the texts of the prayers have been composed in the spirit of African tradition:

The culture of the region has remained basically the oral type. In Black Africa, the word has its art or its force, and it encompasses the qualities of fine language. The African use of word possesses a particular value, thanks to certain stylistic procedures such as the cultivation of sonority, the repetition of words, the use of images, and enigmatic phrases and allusions. It does not encourage monologue; it arouses enthusiasm and favors the participation of the people in the community action.

Ritual dialogue is an essential ingredient of the Zairean liturgy. The presider and the people are in constant dialogue during the worship. In the prayers of the Mass, the homily, and even the eucharistic prayer the African tradition of oral communication is maintained through dialogue. An example is the doxology of the eucharistic prayer, which is usually sung:

Presider:
    Lord, may we glorify your name,

Response:
    Amen.

P: Your name,

R: Amen.

P: Very honorable,

R: Amen.

P: Father,

R: Amen.

P: Son,

R: Amen.

P: Holy Spirit,

R: Amen.

P: May we glorify your name,

R: Amen.

P: Today,

R: Amen.

P: Tomorrow,

R: Amen.

P: For ever and ever,

R: Amen.

There has been consistent effort to introduce intermittent responses in the Mass. A verse of the opening litany will serve as an example:

Presider:
    You, our ancestors of sincere heart,

Response:
    Be with us.

P: You who, aided by God, have served him faithfully,

R: Be with us.

P: Come, let us together glorify the Lord,

R: With all those who celebrate Mass at this time.

On the other hand, the approved text of the Zairean liturgy manifests a certain stiffness with regard to spontaneity. Earlier versions of the text allowed the announcer to appear before the assembly at the beginning of the liturgy, greet the assembly, and then address them spontaneously. This provision has disappeared in the final text. Not only did the Congregation for Divine Worship ask that the actual words of the announcer be made precise in the official text, but the approved text itself is made to read:

The interventions [of the announcer] shall not be improvised, but prepared in advance in writing, and they must aim at presenting the mystery that the church celebrates, proclaimed in the liturgy of the Word, and realized in the eucharistic liturgy.

Here one discerns the Roman influence on the final text of the Mass. The actual practice, however, at celebration is much more relaxed than this rule. The Zairean commission yielded to Roman pressure in the writing of the text, but in the final result this has had little practical consequence.

It is my opinion that the issue of spontaneity was not considered critically by the Vatican authorities in their discussions with the Zaireans. Spontaneity in worship and prayers is not new to Christian life and tradition. It was a common practice in the early church as has been testified to by Justin and Hippolytus. It continues to be an accepted practice in today's Christian churches, including those of Roman Catholic African communities. What is at stake here is not whether spontaneity may be practiced in the church, but under what conditions. There should at least be room for what I term creative or reflective spontaneity. A prayer leader who has taken time to pray, to reflect, and to prepare an upcoming liturgical action may lead effectively without a written text. It is even possible to write out a text, memorize or interiorize the juice of the text, and then pray spontaneously. It could, for example, be used at the greetings of the announcer and presider, at what are officially known as presidential prayers, at the penitential rite, at the prayer of the faithful, and at the closing rite. The ministers who lead at liturgical prayer must have not only the vocation to do so but also the training. When this is the case, they should be free to lead prayer spontaneously . After all, as an African proverb says, "One does not teach the path of the forest to an old gorilla."

Music, Song, and Dance

Missionaries, explorers, and more recently, tourists have been fascinated by the rhythm of tom-toms and other native instruments that fill the Zairean night with intricate sounds. Anyone who leaves the overcrowded cities to journey into the interior of Zaire will still be accosted by the music, song, and dance that are part of the great events of human life in the villages: birth, initiation, marriage, hunting, fishing, communal work, illness, and death. A Missionhurst missionary in Zaire, who had just been present at a wake, wrote:

> I could have hit myself for not having brought a tape recorder or a camera, because what I witnessed was so unique.... Even the buzzing of the fat crickets stopped in the tropical night. Everything was dancing.... Even the bugs and mosquitoes were dancing to the enchanting beat of the drums. Bone and marrow and belly were vibrating together with the trembling earth.... Waves of perspiring and gleaming women's backs undulated around the bier and the women reached for the deceased. A piercing yell in the form of a solo complaint stabbed through the grinding mourning malibu. No one can escape the thrill of such an experience.[26]

Cardinal Jean Danièlou observed:

> I simply do not know how the black people could praise God without dancing, because dancing is so deeply embedded in their whole being that it forms an integral part of their civilization. In them we discover the liturgical meaning of the sacred dance.... They need an incarnation of Christianity which is different and which is in accordance with their instincts and their whole being.[27]

As the famous African philosopher Senghor, said: "The Westerners say: 'I think, therefore I am.' We Africans say: 'I dance, therefore I am.'" Dance in the Zairean liturgy is a natural consequence of living in an environment constantly filled with music.

Practically the entire celebration of the Zairean Mass is sung, with some exception for the proclamation of the Word of God. Even here, the lector, deacon, or priest sometimes chants or sings instead of reading the text. The songs are usually, though not exclusively, sung from memory. Short repetitive verses and choruses are sung to African rhythms, with the accompaniment of musical instruments, hand-clapping, and festive shouts and shrills.

There are five group processions in the Mass — the entrance, the enthronement of the book of the gospel, the presentation of gifts, the communion, and the recessional, and each is accompanied by song, music, and dances. The rubric of the entrance procession says:

> Once the song is begun, a procession is begun from the back of the church. This includes the presider and all those who will minister in any way within that celebration. Each of these other ministers is usually carrying his or her instrument of office. The procession gracefully and slowly moves to the rhythm of the song.

Twice during the celebration, at the Gloria and the Sanctus, there is music, song, and dance around the altar by the ministers. The introduction to the approved text says with regard to the Gloria:

> The dance around the altar by the ministers during the Gloria or a similar song during an incensation shows the desire to commune with the vital force associated with the altar of the sacrifice of Christ.

The "presidential" prayers are shared and sung by the entire assembly. The homily, which is usually a form of dialogue, can become poetic and then lead into a song accompanied by music and dancing. At the thanksgiving song after communion, the whole assembly sings and dances to the rhythm supplied by native and foreign musical instruments. Throughout the Mass, the choir does not sing alone; it leads the assembly in singing.

Music is perhaps one of the most successful aspects of the Zairean liturgy. The people have easily broken away from the inhibitions imported with the Roman Mass and now worship according to their native heartbeats. Since all the songs are native compositions and bear the mark of authentic African rhythms, they are easy for the people to sing even without books.

Nevertheless the theme of joy still needs to be emphasized. Although there is singing and dancing, most of the time the ministers and faithful do not look happy and relaxed. This is a carry-over from missionary catechesis according to which serious faces are the mark of true piety. As little boys, we were cautioned by missionaries and the catechists they trained that we should not move while the priest prayed, even if mosquitoes were sucking us dry! We know better today, and thus, worshipers should be encouraged to feel more at home and relaxed.

Advocating dance in African liturgies is not the same as saying that all forms of dance in Africa are apt for liturgical use. Discernment is called for. "Dance," wrote Bishop Sanon, "is a bodily expression of the spirit.... The expert eye can tell very well if the dancer is dancing for the public, for a third person, or simply turned toward the inner spirit inhabiting him. Without this inhabitation, dance descends into bodily exhibitionism."[28]

There are questions about the distribution of space in the

church to create room for movements and dance. The text of the Zairean Mass does not say anything to this effect, and the matter does not seem to have been discussed. We still have the usual pew arrangement of worship space, and people try to do their singing and dancing from the pews, with everyone virtually imprisoned between kneeler and bench. Free movement is limited to the ministers in the sanctuary space, while the assembly suffocates for want of space. This arrangement does not favor the African worship experience, especially when we think of "dancing space." The worship space in Africa is not just for sitting, standing, and kneeling: it is most essentially for dancing. Open space is therefore an important requirement for African worship. Perhaps the aisle could serve as dancing space during the liturgy. Or better still, more space could be created around the sanctuary so that more people might join the ministers in the dance celebrations.

As the future unfolds, both in Africa and in the African diaspora, worshiping communities should reflect more fully on the importance of liturgical space. Liturgical architects should bear this in mind. Although we have for the most part inherited church buildings designed by people of other cultural backgrounds, the time is here to redesign, rearrange, and re-create our worship space.

Chapter 5

Worship in the Indigenous African Christian Churches

There is one very important worship experience that almost entirely escaped the attention of those who worked on the Zairean liturgy, namely, that of the Indigenous African Christian Churches. These churches are of non–Roman Catholic affiliation and occupy a most prominent place in the Christian experience of sub-Saharan Africa. The progress already accomplished by those spiritually powerful Christian groups is acknowledged infrequently, if at all.

Many members of the highly institutionalized churches in Africa (Roman Catholic, Anglican, Presbyterian, etc.) continue to view the Indigenous Churches (often called "Independent Churches") as inferior and with little theological grounding. Their sacramental systems have been disdained so often and so long that even in those areas of church life in which they have been far more relevant to the local people than their foreign counterparts they have not been well respected. Many official Christian ecumenical groups have not opened their membership doors to these Indigenous Churches.

The emergence of Indigenous African Christian Churches is no longer seen merely as the result of political, social, economic, and racial factors (even though these have played their part), but rather as an answer to a deep "spiritual hunger" among native African Christians. The most significant and unique aspect of these churches is that they seek to fulfill that which is lacking in the Euro-American missionary churches, that is, to provide forms of worship that satisfy both spiritually and emotionally and to address every area of human life and fulfill all human needs.

It will be helpful for us to itemize how liturgical life in these churches has vividly manifested sensitivity toward traditional African values.

Healing

The most important aspect of the worship experience in these churches is their practice of healing. To understand why this practice is central to African experience, we must remember the importance accorded human life in Africa. No assembly is dismissed without some ritual of healing.

Rituals of healing in Africa are usually spectacular and intense. Healers, who may be either men or women, have inherited part of their knowledge from family heritage and traditions. They have also perfected their ministry through continuous practice and experience. Most fundamental, however, is their claim of divine ordination, through which they have been chosen by God to be the agents of grace and life.

Whenever the people gather to celebrate, they gather to heal the sick and strengthen the weak. They practice exorcism as part of the healing process, for among them there is no denying that the devil or evil is very powerful. These healers often recognize certain forms of illness or disability as a manipulation of the devil, and so to heal ultimately involves breaking the hold of the devil on the patient. They invoke the promises of Scripture that Jesus has conquered the power of evil in our world, that Satan has no claim over those who truly believe, and that all things work well for those who love God.

Healers touch their patients continually, laying hands on them and anointing them. Sometimes the patients exhibit signs of possession: for example, vomiting, cursing Christ, fighting the healers, knocking over things around them. It is not unusual to find healers flogging such patients, tying them up with ropes, or forcing potions down their throat to tranquilize them.

In the healing rituals, songs, music, dancing, shouting, commands, and spiritual frenzy are part of the experience. It is in healing rituals that I have seen the most extensive use of African musical instruments, especially the wood-and-leather drum. This instrument is considered the tool of the ancestors, the voice of the spirits, the power of the underworld, the music of the divine. As the drums are beaten, the people clap their hands and dance themselves into frenzy. Soon headaches begin to disappear, bellyaches are forgotten, and energy returns to the weary body.

In most cases those who come to be healed by these healing ministers have already tried all kinds of medication prescribed by hospitals and clinics without positive results. As a last resort, some doctors refer them to these healers and spiritual churches. It is therefore to the credit of these churches that some of these patients are healed. This healing ministry, a fundamental aspect of the preaching of the gospel among African peoples, thus translates despair into hope and life for many families.

Family and Community

The values of family and community are capital in these churches. The members are encouraged to regard each other as members of a family, to support and sympathize with one another. Consequently, the free use of the terms "brother" and "sister" to address one another is common among these churches.

These churches have recaptured the traditional sense of family celebration in their rituals. They hold the family in high esteem when marriages are celebrated. Consent is sought not just from the couple but from the families. The participation of the entire extended family in the life transitions of the new couple is very obvious. The church community lends its energy to the celebrations at the church wedding and beyond.

Respect for age, traditional obligations toward family members, and marriage among members of the community are all encouraged. In this way they maintain a spirit of solidarity.

Wholeness

These churches do not draw any distinctions between the spiritual and the physical aspects of the human person. Instead, they regard the person as a unified whole; any problem affecting the body touches the spirit and vice versa. They give as much time to prayer for emotional and psychological healing as they give to counseling, for example, of alcoholics or the mentally disturbed. There are important ministries of finding food for hungry members, shelter for the homeless, and work for the unemployed, as well as ministries in education and marriage preparation. Every member is ipso facto a minister of some sort, and members contribute their talents and resources for the welfare of the less privileged. The attention given the disadvantaged and despairing members as well as widows, orphans, and the handicapped of the community is a special attraction that flows not only from traditional African sensitivity but also from a conscientious reading of the Bible.

Worship Style

In their style of worship these churches manifest an elaborate use of the human body and its senses. They profess that the human body is beautiful, a gift of the Creator with which people ought to praise and worship. The five senses are deeply engaged in worship with gestures, movements, and symbols.

Yielding the body to the Spirit leads to a sort of "frenzy" that combines dancing, shaking, clapping, singing, prophesying, and speaking in tongues that in some cases seems instrumental in healing and recovery from illness or handicap. Prayers proclaimed during worship in these churches are usually extemporaneous. Even though, on occasion, designated people lead the prayers, generally everyone participates in praying and responding.

Music and Song

Their songs are remarkably short, simple, and repetitive. They are sung responsorially or in multiple spontaneous harmonies. The tempos and rhythms generally follow the beatings of the heart. Singing is normally accompanied by musical instruments (mostly local, but sometimes electronic) deemed worthy for liturgical use.

Their music and singing are generally very loud and highly rhythmic. The words of the songs are almost always drawn directly from Scripture and often from striking stories of the marvels of God in the life of the people of God. These are at the same time song and catechesis. To explain their dancing and music, these churches readily make reference not only to traditional human values, but also to Psalms 149 and 150 and to the incident of David dancing naked before the Lord.

Women

These churches have achieved a high level of integration of women into church life and worship. Some of the most prominent of these Indigenous Churches were founded by women, who go by titles usually picked from the New Testament. Among the Aladura (people of prayer) churches and the Celestial Churches of Christ, for example, women are sometimes the soul and head of the community. They are founders and ritual leaders, much like the priestesses of the many still-surviving traditional cults and shrines. Women are able to perform any ritual act in the community.

Ancestors

These churches invoke the memory of the ancestors, whom they regard not only as the custodians of the unity of the tribe, but also of law, morality, and the ethical order. The history of these churches do not go back primarily to foreign lands, and so even though they may celebrate the memorial of some traditional Christian saints, they more often remember those members of their church community who served well and helped to give a sense of direction and spiritual guidance.

Preaching

Preaching the Word is a powerful tool among these churches. In many cases, they strive to reach out to the widest possible number of people present by using interpreters to go between a widely understood language like English and a local language like Yoruba. The principal ministers in these churches are usually not very sophisticated, but are naturally talented teachers and communicators. When they retell the story of Jesus in the gospels or of the people of Israel in the desert, a listener would almost think that the preacher had been present at the events. They preach as witnesses. Their use of personal testimonies and traditional story forms and imagery very quickly move the people to accepting their message.

When these preachers deal with Scripture passages that contain abstract terms, their ingenuity shines out even the more. On one occasion, a preacher had the task of explaining the term "eternity" to very simple village people. The point of the homily was to describe how long good people will enjoy heaven as a reward for leading good lives on earth. With my own theological background, I was curious as to what he was going to say. Surprisingly, he avoided any philosophical or theological approach. Instead, he pointed to a rock mountain on the horizon. Look at that rock mountain there, he said. We all know how strong and hard it is and how God Almighty placed it there when the world was made. Well, he said, consider that every year, God sends one eagle to fly by this mountain, and the eagle sweeps its wings on it and flies away. Consider how long it will take for those eagles finally to wear away this rock mountain. That is when eternity actually begins. Between now and then is the "jara" (supplemental gift) that God gives good people.

* * * * *

Rather than beginning with a ritual imported by the missionaries and then trying to incorporate aspects of African life into it (I would call this the Africanization of a foreign Christian ritual), the Indigenous African Christian Churches do the opposite: they begin with a native African ritual — which for them is already pregnant with Christian meaning — and then discern biblical idioms and meanings to incorporate into it (this I call the baptism or Christianization of native African rituals). The difference between the former method and the latter is similar to the difference between the "adaptation" and the "incarnation" of worship in post-Vatican II Catholic theology. The former is a form of "transculturation"; the latter is the method of true inculturation as guided by the notion of "incarnation."

In a very special way, therefore, these Indigenous Churches serve as depositories of authentic Africentric worship. It is to them and to other less inhibited, less structured African Christian groups that we must look to find what the Spirit has been saying to the African churches.

Chapter 6

Plenty Good Room: Insights for an African American Thanksgiving

At the end of his monumental work, *The History of Black Catholics in the United States*, the eminent African American church historian Cyprian Davis offers an inspiring "postscript":

The last three decades of the twentieth century witnessed a momentous period of change within the black Catholic community. The number of black Catholics has grown to approximately 1.5 million, with the major centers still being southern Louisiana and the metropolitan areas of New York, Chicago, Washington, D.C., Miami, and Los Angeles. In 1979 the American hierarchy addressed the issue of racism in a pastoral letter, "Brothers and Sisters to Us." Five years later, in 1984, ten black bishops (thirteen by 1988) issued a pastoral letter on evangelization and African American Catholics, "What We Have Seen and Heard." In 1987 the first black Catholic congress in the twentieth century was held in Washington, D.C.; and in the fall of the same year, Pope John Paul gave a special audience to black Catholic leaders in New Orleans. That same year there was created the Black Secretariat in the service of the National Council of Catholic Bishops. Also in 1988, Eugene Marino, the auxiliary bishop of Washington, D.C., was transferred to the See of Atlanta, becoming the first black archbishop in the history of the nation.

As a result of the National Black Catholic Congress of 1987, a national program for evangelization in the black community was drawn up and adopted by the American bishops in 1989. It was a commitment to the African American community and a pledge of support to the zeal of black Catholics. In that same year, a charismatic black priest of the Washington, D.C., archdiocese, George Stallings, launched a call for a separate, semiautonomous status for black Catholics through the formation of an African American rite, or more precisely, an African American ecclesiastical jurisdiction. Disciplined by his ordinary because of the formation of an unauthorized parish, the Imani Temple, George Stallings (who subsequently severed his ties with Rome) and his popular following may well present a challenge and an opportunity to the American church that will be another turning point in its history.[29]

It is especially in and through liturgical celebrations that the identity of any Christian community is defined. Laws, doctrines, and structures have their respective places in the community, but it is through the assembly gathered at worship that the community's beliefs and value systems surface in ritual. Likewise, the Imani Temple phenomenon that Cyprian Davis refers to in his postcript is not so much about doctrinal issues (although these play a part) but about rites and rituals and about sensitivity to the religious and cultural blessings of peoples of African descent in North America. It is about the specific experience of African Americans on the North American continent, a history of slavery and oppression shared by no other ethnic family. It is a history of the woes that have been the lot of the black community in America, but it is also a history that has given birth to blues and gospel and all that characterizes the rich heritage of African American worship.

When George Stallings made his debut outside the organizational structure of the archdiocese of Washington, D.C., he spoke of celebration. He used a text of the Zairean liturgy to launch his Imani Temple experience. In this sense, the Zairean liturgical experience can be said to have influenced the genesis of an African American Catholic liturgical movement.

But that was not the first movement for African American Catholic worship. The 1987 National Black Catholic Congress in Washington, D.C., was clear in its support for liturgical projects for the black Catholic community in the United States, as were many other earlier gatherings. The publication of *Lead Me, Guide Me: The African American Catholic Hymnal* that same year was a major contribution. *In Spirit and Truth: Black Catholic Reflections on the Order of the Mass*, which was published the same year that Rome approved the Zairean eucharistic liturgy (1988), was another step forward. Its goal, according to Bishop Wilton Gregory, was "to review each element of the Order of Mass, describing what choices are permitted or encouraged, and offering commentary on those elements, especially, but not exclusively, for the celebration of the Eucharist in black or predominantly black parishes." The bishop quoted from another episcopal document, *What We Have Seen and Heard:*

We believe that the liturgy of the Catholic Church can be an even more intense expression of the spiritual vitality of those who are of African origin, just as it has been for other cultural groups. ... Through the liturgy, black people will come to realize that the Catholic Church is a homeland for black believers just as she is for people of other cultural and ethnic traditions.[30]

Plenty Good Room: The Spirit and Truth of African American Catholic Worship, issued by the United States Catholic Conference, brought a unique perspective to the movement. Anchored in the biblical theme: "in truth, I see that God shows no partiality. Rather in every nation, whoever fear him and acts uprightly is acceptable to him" (Acts 10:34-35), this document describes the key elements associated with liturgical inculturation in the black Catholic church and also emphasizes the positive value of diversity in the worship. Of special note is its provision of a model for a Sunday eucharistic celebration for an African American Catholic community.[31] In line with these developments, Chicago-based Liturgy Training Publications began publishing *Plenty Good Room* magazine, which is a forum on African American worship in the Catholic Church. Much has been going on, and will even intensify in the years ahead.

Texts have been proposed, but more important are the evolution of new forms of celebration on this continent. At national, regional, and diocesan gatherings, specialized liturgical groups have been called upon to guide participants in the planning and celebration of special liturgies. These have often been memorable experiences and have in fact advanced further than the texts. Audiotapes and especially videotapes have enabled these experiences to be shared far and wide.[32] From these celebrations, many local communities have risen from slumber; Sunday mornings are getting better by the week.

Sharing Gifts

The Zairean liturgy has so much to offer African Americans. It has helped to uncover some of the key aspects of authentic Africanness, which will be crucial in developing African American rituals. But African Americans must also do what many African churches are doing today: sift through the historical data of the past to tap into what is essential, honorable, and good, while abandoning anything that contradicts life and reason.

It is important to realize that certain aspects of African life from many centuries ago are no longer desirable and should not be resurrected: human sacrifice, for instance. Also peoples of African descent around the world must realize that while reaching in to tap the latent energy of our history, we must move on with life wherever we find ourselves. Home is where the Almighty God has placed us now and where we are citizens. African Americans are no longer just Africans but truly African Americans. They are Americans with very deep roots in Africa. They have an unquestionable claim to the heritage of the African continent, but their life is to be sorted out in America. In developing authentic African American rites, therefore, it will be appropriate not only to dip our fingers into the crucible of African worship but also to look very closely at ancient worship on the American continent. The Native Americans share much with African Americans in what concerns the spiritual life and the common experience of suffering and struggle for survival.

Inspiration should also be sought from the entire mosaic of peoples and cultures that make up the entire American family. Every ethnic group in America has blessing in its history and culture, and all of these heritages need to be celebrated. The church should promote the movement toward cultural and social integration. In and through a living Africentric liturgy, a corporate identity, fraternity, and sorority can be celebrated.

The Zairean liturgy offers African American Catholics not the "what" but the "how" of creating models for Africentric liturgical experience. Zaire is distant from the United States not only in physical geographically, but also and especially in cultural, religious, economic, political, and spiritual matters. Zaireans do not have the history of the trans-Atlantic enslavement of their own ancestors; African Americans do. Names like Martin Luther King, Jr., Rosa Parks, Malcolm X, or Sister Thea Bowman,[33] to name a few, do not have much significance to the average person in Zaire; to African Americans, these are sacred icons. In Zaire, the birth of a tiny infant is enough reason for an entire village to initiate a thunderous celebration; in the United States, it may take a world championship in a sporting event to evoke such a parade of grace. In Zaire, all citizens are usually Africans, and the color of the skin is not a point of reference in popular speech; in America, skin color is a capital point of reference, and African Americans are for the most part the oppressed, struggling minority. While millions of Zairean youth stand a good chance of dying of malnutrition and disease, millions of African American youth stand a good chance of dying of gunshots on American streets. So while the text of the Zairean liturgy may be a source of inspiration to African Americans, it cannot and should not become a text for authentic Catholic celebration in America. That is not its purpose.

In my many travels throughout North America, I have been very inquisitive about how people of African descent see the future of their Catholic faith. With the exception of a few isolated cases, African Americans do not desire to have a separate rite that excludes other people. I find this very inspiring, and it is good news for the world's Catholic communion.

After many centuries in the struggle for respectable presence in the Catholic Church, this is not the time for African Americans to quit the struggle and go a separate way. What Pope Paul VI said to African Catholics in Kampala, Uganda, in 1969 can in some way also apply to African Americans today: now is the time to bring out the special gifts, blessings, and values that Almighty God has given you as a people and to share them generously with the rest of the world church. All these thoughts have been brought to life again in the text of *Plenty Good Room.*

To bring a gift to share, one must know precisely what it is that one has received. This search for the identity of African American Catholic blessings has been going on for many years in this country, especially through the efforts of the National Black Catholic Congress and its subsidiary organizations. The National Black Catholic Clergy Caucus, for example, has a committee charged with doing groundwork on an African American eucharistic rite. The word "rite" here is not intended to suggest an independent ecclesiastical entity in the same way we talk of the Roman rite. It is rather an effort to accentuate the special gift of God to peoples of African descent on this continent.

An African American rite will be both broad-based and open-minded. It will embody a special sense of hospitality to other cultures. And yet it will be the place to celebrate the unique gifts of a people whom the Good Lord has brought here to be the conscience of the nation.

In considering what would make an authentic African American worship for our time, we have to pay attention to a history rooted in the forced experience of exodus, pilgrimage, and an intense struggle for survival. Such a worship experience will be a deep community encounter with the core values of African American people on this continent. It will be a celebration fully reflective of the hope that follows despair, of the joy that comes in the morning, of the grace that follows struggle, and of the peace that follows justice. This assembly gathered in the Spirit as a family is on a religious pilgrimage through life, anchored in the strength and legacy of brave and gracious ancestors. The Word will be very important, a powerful proclamation of the creative and saving word through scripture and exhortation. There will be rituals of reconciliation and healing and celebrations of non-violent resistance to injustice and immorality. In song, music, and dance, women, men, and children will praise and glorify God with their total persons as they rise from the dependencies of yesteryear into an affirmed selfhood for today and the days to come. The elderly will receive care, the youth will be instructed, families will be strengthened, and foreigners will find love and hospitality. It will be a time of dedication and worship of God, regulated by the rhythm of the heart rather than the ticking of the clock. This celebration will be an acclamation of salvation in Jesus Christ, all danced in the context of the total meaning of African American spirituality.[34]

Come and See:
A Model of Africentric Celebration

Here I want to propose some ideas, born from my African blood, nourished by my Christian faith, informed by my theological and liturgical experiences, and empowered by a decade of active ministry and celebration in North America. These ideas, I hope, might be useful for those fashioning an authentic African American liturgy – and for those creating other liturgical expressions as well.

Active Participation

The call to full, conscious, and active participation in liturgical celebrations in the document on the liturgy of the Second Vatican Council was certainly inspired by the liturgical experience of the churches of the African continent. Even before that Council gathered, African churches were already requesting Rome to loosen up and let them celebrate according to the sound of life of the people, as we saw when we treated the genesis of the Zairean liturgical experience.

Participation in the assembly plays a great part in the worship of people of African descent. In a typical case of a Sunday eucharistic assembly, there would be an entrance procession in song, music, and dance at the beginning, a gospel procession, a healing ritual procession, a procession of the people to bring gifts to the altar, a procession to share in the communion, and a procession to leave the assembly space after the celebration.

Litany of Saints and Ancestors

A good practice is to have this litany celebrated in three parts. The first is to commemorate some of the saints whose names appear in our popular litanies (parish patrons, family patrons, and others). The people respond with a simple "Pray for us" or "Be with us" following the sung invocation of each name. People in the assembly are invited to invoke names of their family patrons. Some people sing the names out; others proclaim the names aloud. The assembly responds as usual.

The second segment is to introduce names of family members who have passed on. To celebrate my own faith and to lead people into this part of the mystery, I always invoke the names of my father, Alfred, and my youngest brother, Ambrose. There is often a sudden outpouring of names of family members. Some people simply say "my father" or "my wife" without mentioning the name. Most mention them by name. The mourning has not ended yet. For many, the mention of the names makes them weep. This is reality; this is the meaning of the memorial.

The third segment is to introduce names of people around the world who have touched our lives in very deep ways (e.g., Martin Luther King, Jr., Sister Thea Bowman). I have heard people invoke the "little angels of Oklahoma" (referring to the many children who died at the bombing of the Federal building). I have also heard the "martyrs of Rwanda." Sometimes, names of former bishops and pastors are mentioned.

This memorial of saints and ancestors is becoming one of the most powerful experiences in liturgical celebrations. Following a one-week celebration that I had with members of a middle-class white parish in Maryland recently, a pastoral associate wrote me saying:

> Since my father's death in 1972, the Lord has blessed me with a deep conviction of the mystery of the communion of saints. You have helped me deepen my conviction and to release the power of these blessed witnesses into my daily life. Our parish is and will become a more dynamic community because of the experiences you introduced us to.

The Libation

In the context of this ritual of contact and communion with holy ancestors, the assembly can in fact go beyond what is currently being done in many places. For example, it is possible to have a libation rite in communion with the ancestors. A libation is the pouring on the ground of some of the wine used at the ritual to enable the ritual and symbolic participation of the ancestors. Although in many instances in North America, I have seen this ritual performed with water while the litany of saints and ancestors is being sung at the beginning of the celebration, it is more appropriate to have the libation done right before the communion of the faithful. In this case, a piece of the blessed bread and some of the blessed wine can be used instead of water. The libation should be accompanied by prayers addressing the ancestors and inviting them to share in the communion of the pilgrim church.

This proposal may well become the most disputed segment of this model of Catholic celebration. In popular eucharistic catechesis, consecrated elements are not to be thrown or poured out on the ground. But the libation is not just pouring or throwing away consecrated elements. This is ritual and worship. This is communion in the most deeply spiritual sense imaginable. In this unique ritual, the heavens and the earth come into mutual embrace; the pilgrim church and the triumphant church together celebrate and share the ultimate meal of our salvation.

On the other hand, it is important to remember that the consecrated elements do not represent the most important indication of the presence of Christ; the gathered assembly does. In our theology, we have often shifted our attention from people to tiny particles, and while we take great care of the particles, we dishonor people through injustice and negligence.

No one asks that libation be understood by everyone and be practiced by the entire church. But among most Africans in sub-Saharan Africa and many peoples of African descent in diaspora, the ritual of libation is a sacred encounter of the first degree and therefore ought to have its place in any meal assembly of the community.

Ministers and Ministry

Everyone who comes to participate in the church celebration is by that very fact a minister. In the discussions that follow, I intend to take only a sample of liturgical ministers and ministries in order to demonstrate how liturgical planning can make them spiritually richer in the assembly.

Hospitality Ministers: The welcoming spirit, warmth, the healing touch are some of the characteristics of this ministry of love. People are greeted as they arrive. Any visitors are quickly identified and given a special place of welcome in the assembly. Later in the celebration, these guests will be recognized and welcomed by the entire assembly.

Some years ago we developed a rite called "cup of water hospitality." In the weekly liturgy of our International Amen Missioners (IAM) ministry group in Baltimore, we began to have our hospitality ministers welcome people as they arrived for the celebration by serving them a cup of clean, refreshing water. How this ritual was interpreted is noteworthy. For some, it was the physical refreshment; for others the inner healing and therapeutic value were outstanding; for still others the baptismal image, the cleansing theme, the life-giving connotations, or the sign of welcome were most important.

On one occasion when this ritual was performed at a different location without prior catechesis, someone asked why we did it. She pointed to the water fountain at the entrance of the church building and remarked: "People can go there and help themselves if they want to drink water." I explained that many things we do in church are not logical. The reason we serve the water is not because the people cannot help themselves, just as the reason people come together for the Sunday Eucharist is not that they cannot afford bread and wine in their homes. We come together to minister to one another in the Lord and to celebrate. To make this coming together richer is the task of liturgical planning and catechesis.

Welcoming people with a cup of water will remind people of the traditional spirit of hospitality. Among the Igbo of Nigeria, for example, the most fundamental act of hospitality is the serving, blessing, breaking, and sharing of the kola nut. Every welcoming act and every traditional ceremony is begun with it. Every time someone goes to another's home, the kola nut precedes any discussions. In fact, if someone were to visit a family and be treated to a very lavish reception but the serving and sharing of the kola nut were omitted, the person would consider the visit unwelcome. Therefore, if I were preparing a model of assembly and celebration for an Igbo community, I would begin with the presentation, blessing, breaking, and sharing of the kola nut as part of the hospitality rite, followed by the cup of water rite.

Such a ritual could become a most important experience of healing and grace not only in North America but in African churches as well. A cup of clean, refreshing, saving water will be good news to many. Most deaths in many African villages are caused by water-borne diseases. Clean water will be a countersign of that tragic experience of the people.

The Presider: The entire celebration can be hot, cold, or lukewarm in character depending on the person who leads the assembly at worship. It is not just a question of that person's talents, liturgical and theological literacy, academic formation, ability to communicate well, warmth of personality, and spiritual energy; it is a question of all these and especially of a person's faith and conviction.

The presider in the Zairean liturgy carries with him an air of chieftaincy and royalty. He has a commanding presence. This works very well because of values that Zaireans hold important. But it does not mean that presiders in other parts of the world should be the same. Although the theme of service should take precedence over that of power in the role of the primary minister at the eucharistic celebration, it is nevertheless important that the presider maintain a distinctive leadership role that enables and empowers the entire assembly.

In the second part of the eucharistic celebration, the liturgy of the Eucharist, the role of the presider is primary. The eucharistic prayer commands a unique place in the celebration, and, if it is not well presented, it can become a drag on the assembly. A spiritually animated presider, as I have seen in many parts of Africa and elsewhere, will compose verses and responses out of the eucharistic prayers and sing them along with intermittent responses from the people. I have seen the presider and the music ministries sing out the prayers and guide the assembly in its responses in such a way that the entire experience is a solemn memorial and acclamation of the community's faith in the Lord.

When the presider is also the preacher, as is most often the case, the task is multiplied. Personal conviction, experience, and testimony are important aspects of powerful preaching. In the Zairean liturgy, I have seen people other than the presiders called to rise up to preach. At one marriage celebration, a happy couple who recently celebrated their golden wedding anniversary delivered the homily. They had no written texts, nor did they delve into any major theological themes. They shared their life, their struggles and their joys, and especially their hopes and their prayers for the young couple. Everyone learned and cried and rejoiced.

The presider should above all be a happy, spiritually motivated person. The sanctuary is not a space for military exercises. Sometimes, however, presiders arrive looking worn out very early in the morning. Some presiders have confessed entering the sanctuary with pounding headaches and sour emotions because they just watched their favorite sports teams lose a major game on television. We must learn from ritual leaders in some parts of the world who days before they preside over major rites go into a period of personal cleansing and recollection.

Announcer/Animator: The success of the ministry of the announcer in the Zairean liturgy may be due to the relationship of that ministry to that of the traditional town crier. Among people of an oral tradition, it also serves as a ministry of liturgical guidance. In cultures associated with the book and writing, people expect to be given the bulletin or liturgical program so they can read along and know what to expect. But this does not replace the ministry of liturgical guidance.

A man or woman who knows what it takes to build up the spirit of worship in people would be a good minister in this regard. Especially in those communities where people have come to expect a high standard of participation in the celebration, the role of this minister can be a blessing. This minister energizes the community at the very beginning of the celebration and helps the people to "warm up" spiritually. He or she can introduce and prepare the assembly for the healing rituals and processions. The local community will discern at what moments in the celebration this minister should rise and guide the assembly.

Lectors: Those who proclaim the word of God in the assembly bear a mark of major responsibility to the entire community. Rising up to minister in the name of the Lord is an undertaking that requires courage and formation.

Many think that it is enough simply to pick up the lectionary a few minutes before the celebration, look over the text, quickly get the pronunciations right, and then hit the aisle. Sometimes after the lector is seated in the sanctuary in front of the assembly he or she continues to practice the reading while the celebration is going on and so cannot effectively join in the prayers, songs, and acclamations. This becomes a major distraction to many in the assembly and can be a mental obstacle that makes the ministry of the lector ineffective.

On the other hand I have been in parishes where the lectors are chosen for particular celebrations at least four weeks ahead of time. They receive a cassette recording of the scripture text at that time, or they make the recording themselves. During the four weeks they listen to the lection at home or while driving in their cars, and they take time to ponder the message. After a while, the text begins to register and they are able to recall the text from memory. By the day of the celebration, the lector knows the text very well and can in fact proclaim it as story rather than a reading.

The practice of asking for a blessing before proclaiming the Word is a very effective ritual. Whenever it is included in a well planned liturgical celebration, the people are the richer for it.

An elder or announcer can invite the lectors by name out from the assembly. They come forward and stand in front of the assembly. The presider then invites the entire assembly to rise and extend their hands toward the lectors in prayer. Then the presider lays hands on them and leads the community in prayer.

Eucharistic Ministers: Eucharistic ministers are not simply those who assist the priest in distributing holy communion when there are many people present. This ministry has an identity in its own right. Eucharistic ministers should be part of the procession that brings the gifts to the altar during the presentation of gifts. After the gifts have been received at the altar, the eucharistic ministers should stay within the sanctuary, but not crowd around the altar, until it is time for them to perform their ministry. This ministry, which includes both men and women, should embody the theme of family sharing and hospitality in the name of the Lord. Eucharistic ministers should know the physically weak members of the assembly and strive to share communion with them first before going to others.

Cross-Bearer: The Zairean church has built a very strong liturgical case for the ministry of the cross-bearer. What ordinarily is left out in celebrations around the world is here transformed into a major catechetical event. The community considers the cross as the community symbol, somewhat like the national flag, and the bearer is chosen from among the strongest people in the community. The physical strength of the cross-bearer is very evident. This community treasures its symbol of faith and therefore keeps it in the custody of a very strong and reliable person. No one can grab it or steal it away as long as it is in the care of this bearer. After the cross-bearer has placed the cross in the sanctuary, he or she stays by it during the course of the celebration. This is certainly much more liturgically sound than the practice of having a little altar boy or girl bear the cross in procession.

Music Ministries: In many African neighborhoods and villages, Sunday celebration begins in family homes as people get ready to leave for church. Often singing can be heard in the bathroom and as people dress up. The singing increases in volume as the people leave their homes and join with others of the extended family on their way to church. As small groups join with other small groups, the song becomes more elaborate and lively. On the final approach to the assembly place, people leave off singing their own song and join in the song coming from those already in church. All this might begin half an hour or more before the scheduled time for the morning Eucharist.

In many African worship communities, everyone belongs

to the music ministry. Songs are the simple, melodious, repetitious, rhythmic, clappable, danceable choruses that require no books or prior hours of practice. There are thousands of such songs throughout the continent of Africa, many of which are composed in the local languages. These songs are also composed in international languages like English and French, although it is the melody and the music that take precedence over the foreign words. Everybody sings, and in many cases, the "choir" is hard put to make itself heard over the sound of the entire assembly.

Recently I invited parishioners at an affluent middle-class white parish to bring any musical instruments they had in their homes to the parish celebration of the Eucharist at which I was to preside. We surprised ourselves when we arrived with musical instruments from all parts of the world. We picked out songs that people can sing without books, and people played their instruments. The entire assembly joined in the celebration in rhythm and dance. This was not entertainment; we celebrated indeed. We hugged the rest of the evening, and when it was all over, the people returned home with tears of joy and memories that will last forever. The parish discovered so much of what it always had, laid away and waiting to be discovered.

Environment and Art: Since liturgy is not simply an activity of the spirit, the eyes, the nose, the ears, the hands, the feet, the mouth all have to be involved in one way or another for worship to be a unifying experience. What the eyes see, what the ears hear, what the nose smells, what the mouth tastes define the quality of the liturgy. The environment has to be beautiful and appealing: comforting rather than repelling, spiritually uplifting rather than scary or repulsive, inspiring rather than distracting. For example, a sanctuary decorated with rich religious symbols (like the now popular "kente" material[35]) is more likely to move people to sincere worship than a stark and stern classroom environment. The smell of fresh bread is desirable and very acidic wine that bites the tongue is not.

In discussing liturgical architecture, one professor said that "we build a house and, once completed, the house builds us." This is also true of the way liturgical space affects the community of worship. The structure of the church building must be appropriate for the activities that constitute worship when the people are present. The way the chairs are arranged, where the altar is situated, the place of the music ministers during the celebration, the placement of the symbols and items (including the sacramental elements) used for the celebration, all these have their effects on movement and level of participation of the general assembly. The goal is to allow for the maximum interaction between the people as well as free movement space.

With regard to the role of art, I will once again gain inspiration from my contacts with the church in Zaire. During the many months that I joined in the celebrations at the parish church of St. Alphonse in Matete, Kinshasa, I was always drawn into a prayerful mood by the beautiful and powerful traditional art around the sanctuary of the church. The colors and the spiritual images move the worshiper to a sense of awe and worship.

The vestments used in the Zairean liturgy will also inspire anyone who has a sense of the beautiful. In 1981 a Zairean chasuble, a very beautiful, colorful garment designed by local nuns to capture the dignity of the ritual leader, was taken to Nigeria. Soon candidates for priestly ordination in Nigeria had decided to use similar designs for their celebrations. The style has spread to other parts of West Africa. In 1985, samples of the chasuble were taken to North America and were used at major liturgical assemblies. By 1990 several hundred American priests across the country were vesting themselves in chasubles of similar designs. Although people usually require an explanation of the symbols on the chasuble before they can fully appreciate it, most who have commented have said that they prefer this design to any other they have seen.

Africentric Liturgy and Catechesis

It would be very dangerous to surprise a worshiping assembly with a new style of worship one Sunday morning. The Second Vatican Council reminds us that full, conscious, and active participation of the faithful in the celebration is a liturgical right of the assembly. The people need to be fully aware of the various elements of each celebration. This implies that a pastoral liturgical commission needs to develop ways to share with the entire parish community any liturgical developments of the parish. This is the function of catechesis, and the pastor will lead the way in this effort. Without such an effort involving preparation of the people for new liturgical experiences, there could be negative reactions. Right after Vatican II many African people reacted very negatively when they arrived in church one Sunday and, with no prior catechesis, saw the priest looking them in the face instead of turned toward the wall. Some missionaries used such reactions to argue that the people did not want any changes. Years later, we know better.

Outline for an Africentric Liturgy

In this book I have made a conscious effort to avoid verbal prescriptions for exactly what a prayer leader, presider, or other minister should say at any given time in the celebration. If that were to be needed, it would be another project altogether. Nonetheless, every prayer leader ought to be well prepared for his or her ministry. Those who lead the prayers must know what constitutes the type of prayer that they are to lead.

Here I want to propose an outline for a Sunday eucharistic celebration, hoping that the reasons behind any new elements in this model are clear from what I have already said.

The Gathering

The music ministers, already in place, explode in music and song. They invite arriving members to participation. Hospitality ministers welcome people as they arrive and help them to feel part of the family.

- Cup of water hospitality (as people arrive)
- Welcome by an elder and hospitality to new members

When the time approaches to begin the procession, a church elder goes to the sanctuary and welcomes all.

- Call to worship by an announcer
- Songs of praise for procession
- Ritual procession: cross-bearer (visibly strong person), incense bearers, musicians, ritual dancers, ministers bearing instruments of ministry, presider, acolytes, people with testimonies (for example, birth, marriage, graduation)
- Litany of saints and ancestors
- Brief testimonies, at the sanctuary (each testimony may be received by singing: "He has done great things for me…")
- Gathering prayer

Liturgy of the Word

- Prayer over the ministers of the Word
- Proclamation of the Word

- Gospel processions and acclamation
- Proclamation of the gospel
- Preaching
- Penitential rite and healing: reconciliation prayers, petition prayers, healing prayers, blessing of oil, anointing and laying on of hands
- Joyful sharing of peace greeting

Liturgy of the Eucharist

- Procession with thanksgiving gifts
- Presentation of gifts with prayers
- Ritual designation of gifts for the poor
- Eucharistic Prayer
- Lord's Prayer
- Breaking of bread
- Libation
- Communion of the faithful
- Thanksgiving and prayer

Rite of Sending Forth

- Concluding announcements
- Blessing and sending forth
- Dance of the assembly into life

Conclusion

Where Do We Go from Here?

There is more than one way of assessing the style and the degree of inculturation of the Zairean Mass. In this study we have chosen primarily the method of assessing its incorporation of traditional African values. We have looked at the text and celebration of the rite to see if the Zairean commission has taken advantage of the openings made by Vatican II's Constitution on the Sacred Liturgy in December 1963. We end our study with a mixed reaction.

We can rightly say that the Zairean Mass has moved the development of African Christian liturgies much further than any other single liturgical venture on the continent. A greater awareness of African values has been demonstrated, although more in the celebration itself than in the approved text. The dialogue for greater development of the rite continues as more African theologians and liturgists react to what they see in the Zairean liturgy.

We have evaluated the rite on the basis of the published text and the way it is celebrated in Kinshasa. It is possible, of course, that somewhere in Zaire's interior communities may have gone way ahead of Kinshasa. The future growth of the

Zairean Mass could be more interesting in those communities, where the primary reference is the celebration itself rather than the text.

The Zairean Mass is unique for several reasons. First, initiated by a local conference of bishops and developed through full dialogue with Rome, it is the first full indigenous rite of the Eucharist approved by Rome since Vatican II.

Second, as an African celebration of the Eucharist, it stands in a class of its own, easily distinguished from text-only proposals such as the "All Africa Eucharistic Prayer." The Zairean Mass is both text and celebration.

Third, the Zairean Mass is the one African liturgical experience evoking the widest interest, ranging from that of ordinary Christians to theologians, liturgists, and bishops. It has therefore had broad exposure to critique and scholarly appreciation.

Fourth, the Zairean Mass has demonstrated more sensitivity to traditional African values than other official eucharistic rites of Roman affiliation. It was the first to invoke the memory of African ancestors in the context of Catholic worship; it also gave a prominent role to the announcer, whose ministry reflects that of the village town crier. The Zairean Mass is the most inculturated liturgical experience in Catholic Africa today.

People familiar with the liturgical experience in Zaire today testify that the celebration itself is far more Zairean than the text. According to the testimony of the bishops of the land, the dreams of Vatican II are being realized in the Zairean liturgical experience:

> On the one hand, the active participation of the faithful, and on the other hand, the spontaneity with which they respond and pray, are a witness that this rite responds to the need for a tangible and interior religious manifesta-

tion on the part of the people of Zaire. In fact, a greater
understanding of the mystery of Christ the Redeemer is
being achieved. Besides, there is a deeper awareness that
the eucharistic celebration is a festive action of the Christian community.... People go to Mass, not because it is
required of them, but because they have discovered that
the assembly is the place where one meets God and one's
brothers and sisters. It is there that the human religious
sentiment is satisfied at the level of affectivity, aesthetics,
and in solidarity with others.... It is at the origin of a new
form of realizing the presence of God, the brotherhood of
the faithful, and their engagement in the world.[36]

Nevertheless, there is more work to be done with this celebration, what has been referred to often as the need to go
much further ("aller plus loin"). All is not well yet with the
Rite Zairois. The diocesan liturgical commission believed that
Vatican II did not envision the creation of a new family of rites,
an interpretation that is now being questioned. Some say that
the problem is not with the text of the Vatican document itself,
but with official interpretations of its provisions by the Roman
Curia. At the local level, theologians and liturgists see more
possibilities in the Constitution on the Liturgy than some conferences of bishops have so far allowed. Moreover, the church
has moved beyond Vatican II.

The discussions concerning the inculturation of the gospel
around the world have broadened the church's vision of its
mission. More options now exist for evangelization in Africa
than in 1969 when the groundwork for the Zairean Mass was
begun. There is a need to re-evaluate the basic assumptions
made in the composition of the text. Most of the criticisms
raised by African theologians refer to Roman dependence, for
example, the Roman *Ordo* as a basis for the liturgy. There
is need to reconsider the models used; the role of the male

village chief, for example, is self-limiting. There should be more reflection on the nature of African rituals of assembly, offerings, and sacrifices. There is need for more sensitivity to traditional values and their various ritual expressions. The evolution of the rite must continue.

Some of the omissions in the Zairean Mass are surprising, at least to anyone who shared the initial dreams of the Zairean bishops. Why, for example, is there so little concern for issues of human life and its promotion? The silence on healing and the lack of commitment to social justice in the Mass are clearly regrettable.

Some ask, Is the Zairean Mass a different "rite" or is it what the approved text calls it: "Missel Romain pour les Dioceses du Zaire"? The Zairean Mass is different from the Roman Mass in many ways. It is therefore more than a "missel romain" for Zaire. At the same time, it represents only one aspect of what constitutes a "rite" and so it is not to be seen as a rite in itself. A full rite in Zaire would include the entire sacramental system, as well as other aspects of church life and practice. These other areas are part of the future project of the bishops conference of Zaire. The goal, however, is not for an independent rite in Zaire.

The result of the give-and-take between the Roman Congregations and the Zairean bishops and their commissions led to a modest and conservative liturgical rite (as far as the text is concerned). The Zairean Mass is neither the Roman Mass known to most of us, nor is it the Zairean dream-made-flesh that we came to expect. It is a kind of hybrid: its blood is Roman, but the flesh is African.

In Kinshasa I was also asked if the Rite Zairois is truly national, or is it a "Rite Kinois"? (The term "kinois" refers to someone or something from Kinshasa.) It was essentially kinois because of the central role that Cardinal Joseph Malula of Kinshasa played in its development. In Kinshasa the Parish of St. Alphonse of Matete is still the main center, with the cathedral church in Kinshasa playing an important role on major feast days, especially when the presider is the bishop. A majority of the bishops of Zaire, however, are behind the development of the Zairean Mass. According to information gathered from students at the Faculté de Théologie Catholique de Kinshasa in 1989, it is celebrated in most of the dioceses. In different places, however, there is variation, for example, in the extent and style of dance. The language is also different from the Lingala used in the celebration at Kinshasa.

The Zairean Mass has already filtered beyond the national boundaries of Zaire. In 1981, I made key modifications to parts of the celebration, and we celebrated it as our Sunday liturgy at the Dominican community in Ibadan, Nigeria. Since then, it has been used in various forms by Dominicans in Nigeria. I have also used significant parts of it at Sunday liturgies in various places in the United States. People who visit Zaire are returning with videotapes and recordings of the Zairean Mass. The text of the Mass receives attention in international liturgical and cultural reviews. A feature in *Time* magazine on African religious art included photographs taken during the celebration of the Zairean Mass in Kinshasa. I have personally received requests from many pastors in North America, asking for a copy of the text of the Zairean Mass.

But where do we go from here? The Zairean Mass has been approved, but now that its pioneer advocate, Cardinal Malula of Kinshasa, has passed away, what will become of this liturgical experience? Will the Zairean church take further steps in favor of inculturation or will it be intimidated? Will other churches of Africa follow the signal in Zaire? Will other church communities of peoples of African descent around the world pick up their mats and dance along the path of authenticity in worship? These questions can be answered only with the passage of time. For one thing, those who think that things move slowly in Africa are right; for more than a year after the approval of the text of the Zairean Mass, there was no complete published copy of it anywhere. The local press continued to "put things together." To ensure a more positive outcome in the near future, this is the time for African theologians and liturgists to rally around the commission working on the Zairean Mass to help this celebration gain greater maturity.

The Zairean Mass as it now stands is not for export, whether to nearby Burundi or the faraway United States. It was never intended for that purpose. No local liturgy should be packaged for export. It has taken us centuries to recognize this fact. However, it would be presumptuous for anyone to attempt to develop an authentic eucharistic celebration for any African peoples without prayerfully and studiously approaching the text and celebration of the Zairean Mass. Much groundwork has been done in the two and a half decades of its evolution. What the Zairean church has accomplished should be used as a point of departure for the other African churches, and it is to the actual celebration rather than the text that attention should be given.

For peoples of African descent who are either pilgrims or sojourners in other parts of the world, this African liturgical experience should serve as an invitation to rise up and dance. It is part of our religious testimony, and we should donate whatever is good and honorable in our faith experience to the world church. We sing, clap, dance, and celebrate; this is our story, our song, and our testimony.

Our goal will be met if this study helps to move the Zairean Mass toward maturity and if other local churches of Africa, and indeed the rest of the Christian world, are inspired, through the power of the Spirit, to develop authentic ways of celebrating the Lord's Supper reminiscent of the dynamism with which the Word of God took human flesh to dwell among us.

Appendix

A Text of the Solemn Zaïrean Rite of the Eucharistic Liturgy

[This text is taken from *Communautés et Liturgies* 62 (1980): 57–76. The published text is in French; the translation is mine. I include this earlier version of the Zaire liturgy because it is much closer to what the church in Zaire wanted—closer than the final text approved in 1988. This is not the final text approved in 1988. The approved text, however, is usually cited elsewhere in this book.]

Arrival at Place of Worship

The people arrive from their various homes and exchange greetings. Each one normally brings something for the offering. In fact, "it is proper for the faithful to show their participation by bringing either the bread or the wine for the celebration of the Eucharist, or other gifts that will be used to sustain the Church and its needy members" (*Ordo Missae*, no. 13).

141

Opening of the Eucharistic Celebration

The Announcer Enters

When the time has come to begin the celebration, the announcer — man or woman — wearing a proper, distinctive vestment, goes to the front of the assembly. He/she strikes an instrument (often a gong), which symbolizes a call to silence. Standing by the lectern, he/she greets the assembly in these terms:

Announcer:
> Brothers and sisters
> May the grace, mercy, and peace from God our Father
> and from Jesus Christ our Lord
> be with you all.

All: Amen.

Then he/she announces that the Mass is now about to begin. He/she introduces the celebrants (presider and concelebrants), and then any special guests who have come to join in the community's celebration. Asking the people now to rise up, he/she invites them to join in singing the opening song, which the choir now intones. He/she then goes to his/her proper place.

Entrance of the Celebrant

Once the song is begun, a procession is begun from the rear of the church. This includes the presider and all those who will minister in any way within the celebration. Each of these other ministers is usually carrying his/her instrument of office. The procession gracefully and slowly moves to the rhythm of the song.

Veneration of the Altar

On arriving at the sanctuary, the assisting ministers form a semicircle around the altar, thus facing the people. The presider (and any other concelebrants) then turn around at the altar, facing the people. All of them then greet the altar by a deep bow, genuflection, or prostration. The presider may also stand by the center of the altar with his hands extended in a "V" form. Then he inclines toward the altar, his face touching it. He then repeats this gesture at the other three sides of the altar, moving around to the right. Meanwhile, the other ministers remain bowed low.

The presider may bless some incense and put some of it on the charcoal fire already placed near the altar. The rising smoke may well symbolize the prayers of the faithful rising to the Father (cf. Ps. 141:2).

After the veneration of the altar, each person goes to his/her proper place.

Presider's Opening Message

When the people have stopped singing, the presider greets them. He then indicates the principal theme of the celebration, usually taken from the content of the biblical passages to be read.

Invocation of Saints

Then the celebrant, in the following words, invites the people to unite themselves to all those who have returned to God and are now resting in the peace of Christ.

Presider:
>   My brothers and sisters, we who are alive on earth today are not the only followers of Christ. Many have

already left this world and are now with God. Some did not even know or hear of Christ in their lifetime. But if they sought God with a sincere heart and were even aided by God to do God's will, then they too are with God. Together with all of these saints, we form one great family. Let us now join ourselves to them. May this sacrifice gather all of us into one family.

After a brief period of silence for the sake of interiorization, the assembly prays the following invocations:

Presider:

   Holy Mary Mother of God,

All: Be with us.

P: You who are the Mother of the Church,

A: Be with us.

P: Come, let us together glorify the Lord

A: With all who celebrate Mass at this time.

P: St. N ... (patron of the parish),

A: Be with us.

P: You who are the patron of our parish

A: Be with us.

P: Come, let us together glorify the Lord

A: With all who celebrate Mass at this time.

P: St. N ... (saint of the day),

A: Be with us.

P: You whom we venerate on this day,

A: Be with us.

P: Come, let us together glorify the Lord

A: With all who celebrate Mass at this time.

P: All you saints of heaven,

A: Be with us.

P: You whose names we bear,

A: Be with us.

P: Come, let us together glorify the Lord

A: With all who celebrate Mass at this time.

P: And you our (righteous) ancestors

A: Be with us.

P: You who, aided by God, have served God faithfully,

A: Be with us.

P: Come, let us together glorify the Lord

A: With all who celebrate Mass at this time.

People's Acclamation

Recognizing that the assembly of all those united in Christ is a sign of the presence of the kingdom, the people sing a song of glory and praise to God. The presider (or another minister) now adds more incense to the fire. Depending on the liturgical time, the Gloria or any other appropriate song may be sung. The people dance to the rhythm of the song in their places, while the celebrant and all the ministers dance around the altar.

Opening Prayer

After the acclamation, the presider invites the people to prayer in these words:

P: Brothers and sisters,
let us raise our hands in prayer.

All the people raise up their hands. Then, after a brief moment of silence, the presider says or sings the opening prayer. The people conclude the prayer by responding "Amen." However, in some places where it is the practice, the conclusion to the prayer, that is, "Through our Lord Jesus Christ your Son..." may be said or sung by all the people.

Liturgy of the Word

After the opening prayer, the assembly is seated. The reader approaches the presider, bows before him, and asks for blessing and authority to proclaim the Word.

Reader:
> O priest of God, bless me.
> May the Lord be with me.
> May I proclaim the Word of God well.

The presider imposes his hands on his/her head and prays:

P: May the Lord help you.
> May your eyes see well.
> May your word console the hearts of our people.

The reader responds with "Amen" and shows a sign of gratitude. He/she then goes to the lectern.

Proclamation of the Word

The reader first introduces the reading briefly. He/she announces the passage in the Bible from which the reading is taken, and then proclaims it. At the end, one of the following acclamations is made:

Reader:
> Brothers and sisters,
> this is the Word of God.

A: We accept it.

OR

Reader:
Whoever has ears to hear,

A: Hear!

Silence or Song of Response

After the reading, the announcer may invite the assembly to reflect in silence. Otherwise, a meditative song appropriate to the celebration may be sung. When there is a second reading, everything is as indicated for the first. This reading is followed by an acclamation of the people.

Enthronement of the Gospel

The presider or whoever will proclaim the gospel adds more incense to the fire and then prays the "Munda Cor." As he takes up the gospel book from the altar, the candle-bearers join him. The announcer joins them with his/her gong. Now facing the people, they process to where the gospel will be proclaimed. First, the book of the gospel is presented to the people with this dialogue.

P: My brothers and sisters,
the Word of God became flesh.

A: And he dwelt among us.

P: Let us listen to him.

The people sing the Alleluia verse or other enthronement song. Meanwhile, the gospel procession moves toward the lectern. The announcer leads while joyously sounding the gong. When they arrive at the lectern the announcer says to the people:

Announcer:
> Brothers and sisters,
> let us lend our ears.

A moment of silence follows. Then the presider or gospel-proclaimer says:

P: The Good News as St. N ... has written it.

A: Glory to you, O Christ, glory to you.

> OR

> Announce it, announce it, we are listening.

Then the people sit (in most places) for the proclamation of the gospel. At the end, the following conclusion is made:

P: He who has ears to hear

A: Let him hear.

P: He who has the heart to accept

A: Let him accept.

The homily follows. It is given by the presider or, in some cases, by an appointed elder.

Profession of Faith

When it is required by liturgical law, the Credo is said.

The Penitential Act

After the profession of faith or the homily (whichever is the case), the presider invites the people to an act of penance in these or similar words.

P: Brothers and sisters,
> the Word of God has enlightened us.
> This Word is ever active.

It can judge the feelings
and the thoughts of our hearts.
We know that we have not always
followed its demands
And yet everything is clear to the eyes of God.
Let us ask the Lord to give us the strength
that we may walk on his way.

There is a silent pause; then the people express their sorrow by taking up an attitude of repentance: standing with head bowed and hands crossed on the breast. Then the following invocation is humbly said or sung.

P: Lord our God,
as the blood-sucker sticks unto our skin
and sucks our blood,
evil has come upon us.
Our life has been diminished.
Who can save us, if not you, Our Lord?
Lord have mercy.

A: Lord have mercy.

P: Before you, O Blessed Virgin Mary,
before you, all the saints,
before our brothers and our sisters
we confess that we have done wrong
and that our hearts have been far from you.
We have worshiped you only with our lips.
Christ have mercy.

A: Christ have mercy.

Then the presider goes around and sprinkles the assembly with holy water. During this time, a song with the baptismal theme is sung. When he returns to his place, he concludes with the following prayer:

P: Most Holy Father, hear our prayer:
          may our hearts not be inclined to evil;
          forgive our faults,
          because of the sacrifice of your Son Jesus Christ.
          May your Spirit dwell in our hearts
          and may our sins be cleansed
          in the deep and silent waters of your mercy
          through Jesus Christ our Lord.

A: Amen.

Sharing of the Gift of Peace

The presider invites the assembly to share the peace in these words:

P: Brothers and sisters,
          in the love of Christ,
          let us give the peace to one another.

The one who gives peace says, "The peace of Christ." The one who receives says, "Yes, peace!"

Prayer of the Faithful

One of the ministers may add some incense to the fire. As the smoke rises the intentions of the assembly are offered up.

Liturgy of the Eucharist

Bringing of Gifts

Before the Mass, the ciboria are filled with eucharistic hosts; a little water is also added to the wine in the chalice. These are placed on a little table either at the rear of the church or in some other convenient place. Other gifts brought by the people are placed next to these. When the offertory song is begun, those designated to present the gifts go to carry them. Then, dancing to the rhythm of the song, they advance in procession toward the altar. Depending on the place, they may be accompanied by acolytes. At the entrance of the sanctuary, the presider meets them. The people stop singing.

The Presentation of Gifts

The offerings of the people (other than the bread and wine) are first presented to the presider by one of those carrying them, saying:

> O priest of God,
> here are our gifts.
> Receive them.
> They show our spirit of solidarity and sharing
> and that we love one another
> as the Lord has loved us.

The presider thanks them with a gesture. Then he receives the gifts and hands them over to the assisting ministers. The gifts are then put in their proper place. Those carrying the hosts and the wine address the presider in these terms:

> O priest of God,
> here is the bread,
> here is the wine,
> gifts of God.
> They also come from the fields
> and from our human efforts:
> Receive them.
> Do offer them to our God
> that they may become food for eternal life.

The presider also thanks them. Then he receives the hosts and the wine. The other ministers help him to put these on the altar, as those who brought the gifts return to their places.

The Offering of the Oblation

The presider may now incense the gifts and the altar and wash his hands. Then he invites the people to prayer, saying:

> Brothers and sisters,
> let us raise our hands in prayer.

The people rise and raise their hands for prayer. The presider takes the chalice with his right hand and the container of the large host with his left. He raises these up to eye level, and then says or sings the prayer over the gifts. The people join in the conclusion as indicated for the opening prayer. Then the presider places the chalice and the paten back on the altar.

The Eucharistic Prayer

Initial Dialogue

The announcer strikes his/her gong and says to the people:

> Brothers and sisters,
> let us listen attentively.

All remain in silence for a moment. Then a dialogue begins between the presider and the people.

P: The Lord be with you

A: And with your spirit.

P: Let us raise our heart.

A: We turn our heart to the Lord.

P: Let us give thanks to the Lord our God.

A: Truly, it is right (to do so).

Theological Section

P: Truly, Lord,
it is good that we give you thanks,
that we glorify you,
you, our God,
you, our Father,
you, the sun we cannot fix our eyes upon,
you, sight itself,
you, the master of all peoples,
you, the master of life,
you, the master of all things,
we give you thanks
through your Son Jesus Christ, our mediator.

A: Yes, he is our mediator.

Christological Section
(an adaptation of Eucharistic Prayer II)

P: Holy Father,
we praise you through your Son
Jesus Christ our mediator.
He is your Word who gives life.
Through him you created heaven and earth;
through him you created the streams of the world,
the rivers, the ponds, the lakes,
and all the fishes that dwell in them.
Through him you created the stars,
the birds of the sky, the forests,
the plains, the savannas, the mountains,

and all the animals that dwell therein.
Through him you have created
all the things that we see,
and all that we do not see.

A: Yes, through him, you created all things.

P: You made him master of all things.
You sent him among us
that he may become our Redeemer and Savior.
He is God made man.
By the Holy Spirit,
he took flesh from the Virgin Mary.
We believe it to be so.

A: We believe it to be so.

P: You sent him
that he may gather all men (and women)
that they may form one single people.
He obeyed,
he died on the cross,
he conquered death,
he rose from the dead.

A: He rose from the dead,
he conquered death.

P: This is why
with all the angels,
with all the saints,
with all the dead who are with you,
we say (sing): You are holy.

The Trisagion

A: Holy! Holy! Holy!
Lord, God of the universe,
heaven and earth are filled with your glory.

Hosanna in the highest heavens.
Blessed is he who comes in the name of the Lord.
Hosanna in the highest heavens.

The Trinitarian Embolism

P (and concelebrants):

Lord our God, you are holy.
Your only Son, our Lord Jesus Christ, is holy.
Your Spirit, the Paraclete, is holy.
You are holy, almighty God.
We pray you, listen to us.

Pre-consecratory Epiclesis

As may be appropriate, the presider and the concelebrants extend their hands over the oblation while pronouncing the following words:

Look at this bread,
look at this wine,
look at them.
Sanctify them:
May the Holy Spirit descend on these offerings
that we bring before you.
May they become for us
the body and blood of our Lord Jesus Christ.

Words of Institution

P (and concelebrants):

The same night that he was arrested,
he took bread,

The presider takes the bread and holds it up for the people to see. Then he continues:

> He praised you,
> he implored you,
> he gave you thanks,
> he broke the bread
> and gave it to his disciples, saying:
> Take and eat, all of you,
> this is my body.
> I deliver it for you.

Some ringing of the bell may accompany the entire words of institution. The presider shows the host to the people. The people may respond with an acclamation. The host is placed back on the altar. Then the presider (and concelebrants) genuflect or bow low without holding the altar. Rising again, they continue.

> So also, at the end of the meal,
> he took the cup.

The presider takes the cup.

> He praised you,
> he implored you,
> he gave you thanks,
> he gave it to his disciples, saying:
> Take and drink, all of you,
> for this is the cup of my blood,
> the blood of the new and everlasting covenant.
> It will be for you and for all people
> the remission of sins.
> Do this for my remembrance.

The presider shows the cup to the people. They may respond with an acclamation. Having put the cup back on the altar, the presider (and concelebrants) genuflect or bow low without holding the altar. As he rises, the presider says:

P: It is great, the mystery of faith.

A: You have died.
We believe it.
You have risen.
We believe it.
You will return in glory.
We believe it.

P (and concelebrants):
Lord our God,
we remember the death and resurrection of your Son.
We offer to you the bread of life.
We offer to you the cup of salvation.
We thank you for making us your chosen ones
worthy to serve in your presence.

Post-Consecratory Epiclesis

P (and concelebrants):
Lord God of mercy,
behold, we shall eat the body of Christ;
we shall drink the blood of Christ.
We therefore ask you:
Have mercy on us.
Send your Spirit upon us.
May your Spirit gather us together.
May we become one.

A: Lord, may your Spirit gather us together.
May we become one.

Intercessions

The presider (or concelebrant) makes the following intercessions in dialogue with the people.

P: Lord, remember your church.
       Its presence is felt all over the world.
       May all Christians love one another, as you love us.
       Remember the pope....
       Remember our bishop....
       Remember those who are faithfully guarding
          over the apostolic faith.
       Remember those who govern the nations.

A: Lord, remember all of them.

P: Lord, remember our brothers (and sisters)
       who have died in the hope of resurrection,
          or of salvation.
       Remember them all.
       Remember all those who have left this earth,
       whose hearts you know.
       Remember all of them.
       Receive them in your presence.
       May they behold your face.

A: Lord, remember all of them.

P (or concelebrant):
       Lord, we pray you,
       remember all of us.
       May we be received in your presence some day,
       where you dwell with the blessed Virgin Mary,
       mother of God,
       the Apostles and the saints of all ages,
       all those whom you love and who have loved you.
       May we then be in your presence

to praise and glorify you
through your Son, Jesus Christ, our Lord.

Final Doxology

The presider and concelebrants raise the bread and the cup and sing:

P: Lord, may we glorify your name!

A: Yes.

P: Your name!

A: Yes.

P: Very honorable!

A: Yes.

P: Father!

A: Yes.

P: Son!

A: Yes.

P: Holy Spirit!

A: Yes.

P: May we glorify it!

A: Yes.

P: Today!

A: Yes.

P: Tomorrow!

A: Yes.

P: For ever and ever!

A: Yes.

The Communion

The Lord's Prayer

Having placed the bread and the cup back on the altar, the presider addresses the people thus:

P: As we have learnt from the Lord
and as he has commanded,
we dare to say.

OR

Brothers and sisters,
children of the same Father,
let us ask to live in unity,
we who shall eat the same bread.

All the people stand, and with hands raised, say or sing the Our Father.

Embolism of the Lord's Prayer

The presider says or sings:

P: Lord,
deliver us from all evil, we pray you;
give us peace, we pray you.
In your mercy, free us from sin, we pray you;
give us your courage and your patience
in the midst of the trials that we encounter in this life.
Come and help those who hope
in the goodness that you promise,
those who await the coming of our Savior, Jesus Christ.

A: To you be the reign,
to you be the power,
to you be the glory,
for ever and ever.

Breaking of Bread

Here the presider breaks the bread. He puts a fragment of it in the chalice, saying in a low voice:

P: The body and blood of Christ are reunited in this cup. May they give us everlasting life.

Meanwhile, the people say or sing:

A: Lamb of God, who takes away the sin of the world have mercy on us. (twice)
Lamb of God who takes away the sins of the world, grant us peace.

Prayer before Communion

The presider prays in a loud voice:

P: Lord Jesus Christ, Son of the living God,
according to the will of the Father
and with the power of the Holy Spirit
you died that the world may have life.
By your body and blood, deliver us from our sins;
deliver us from all evil.
Help us to keep your commandments;
may we never be separated from you.

OR

Lord Jesus Christ,
we shall share your body and blood.
May this communion bring us neither judgment nor condemnation;
instead, let it uphold us,
and become the remedy that brings us healing.

Communion

The presider bows low. Then, he takes the consecrated bread and shows it to the people, saying:

P: Happy are those invited to the Lord's meal.
Here is the lamb of God
who takes away the sin of the world.

A: Lord, I am not worthy to receive you,
but only say a word
and I shall be healed.

Then the presider says in a low voice (if there are concelebrants, each one receives a piece of consecrated bread):

P: May the body of Christ keep me (us) unto eternal life.

He/they eat(s) the body of Christ. Then the presider takes the chalice and says in a low voice:

P: May the blood of Christ keep me (us) unto eternal life.

The priest takes the ciborium and approaches the people who come forward to communicate. He shows the consecrated bread to each one, saying:

P: The body of Christ!

The communicant responds:

A: Amen!
OR
I believe!

The communion song is begun while the priest is taking communion. After the distribution of communion, the priest or the deacon purifies the paten and the chalice. (This may also be done after the Mass). The presider may return to his seat. A period of silence may follow or otherwise a song (of thanksgiving) may be sung.

Concluding Prayer

The presider invites the people to prayer in these words:

P: Brothers and sisters,
let us raise our hands up in prayer.

All the people rise and take a position of prayer. There is a brief moment of silence. Then the presider says or sings the prayer, to which the people conclude with an "Amen."

Concluding Rite

At this point, the announcer makes any announcements for the week ahead. Then there is the blessing and sending forth.

P (and concelebrants):
May the Master of life,
the Father, the Son, and the Holy Spirit,
keep you for ever and ever.

A: Amen!

The exit from the church is a joyous moment. The ministers process out dancing to the rhythm of the closing song; the people follow.

Notes

1. Edward Braxton, "An African Church for African People," in *America* (November 24, 1984): 342-43.

2. Brian Hearne, "The Significance of the Zaire Mass," *AFER* 17 (1975): 219.

3. "Cameroon: A Dance before the Lord," *Missionhurst* (June-July 1972): 20-12.

4. Ralph E. S. Tanner, *Transition in African Beliefs* (New York, 1967), 122.

5. William Callewier, "More Than Adaptation," *Missionhurst* (August-September 1969): 4-5.

6. Anselme Sanon, "Cultural Rooting of the Liturgy in Africa since Vatican II," in Mary Collins and David Power, eds., *Concilium* 162 (1983): 65.

7. Pope Paul VI, "Closing Discourse to All-Africa Symposium," *Gaba Pastoral Papers*, no. 7 (1969): 50-51. See also Aylward Shorter, *African Christian Theology: Adaptation or Incarnation?* (London: Geoffrey Chapman, 1975), 20.

8. "Synod Bishops from Africa Issue Declarations," *AMECEA Documentation Service*, no. 11 (February 1974): 2-3.

9. The final document of the Extraordinary Synod, in *The Tablet* (December 14, 1985): 1328.

10. Conference Episcopale du Congo, "Apostolat liturgique — Adaptation du culte," in *Actes de la VIe Assemblée Plénière de l'Episcopat du Congo* (Leopoldville: Secretariat Général de l'Episcopat, 1961), 362-63.

11. "Congo: A Long and Arduous Road," *Missionhurst* (August-September 1971): 22-24.

12. Elochukwu Uzukwu, "Inculturation of Eucharistic Celebration in Africa Today," *CHIEA: African Christian Studies* (Nairobi, Kenya) 1 (1985): 19–20.

13. Ibid., 18.

14. *La Documentation Catholique* 85 (1988): 649.

15. "Presentation générale...," no. 14, in *Notitiae* 24 (1988): 459.

16. As in the approved text of 1988, in *Notitiae* 24 (1988): 465.

17. "Presentation générale...," no. 14, in *Notitiae* 24 (1988): 461.

18. Commission Episcopale de l'Evangelization, *Ordo Missae Zairensis cum Populo* (Schema normatif, 1st edition), 1.

19. See B. Jarczyk, "Msgr. Sanon, Evêque du Burkina-Faso: L'amour avant le pardon," in *La Croix* (December 8–9, 1985): 16.

20. From the approved text (1988).

21. Albert Feys, as reproduced in *Missionhurst* (June–July 1972): 7.

22. Mpoto M. L. Mpongo, "Le 'rite Zairois': Quelques-unes de ses caracteristiques," in *Mediations africaines de sacré,* Actes du troisième Colloque International, Kinshasa, November 16–22, 1986 (Kinshasa: Faculté de Théologie Catholique, 1987), 512.

23. From the 1988 approved text.

24. From the 1988 approved text.

25. Charles Vandame, in *La Croix,* December 6, 1985, 7, cited by Mpongo, "Le 'rite zairois,'" 513.

26. As described in "Congo: From Rural Tom-Tom to Urban Orchestra...and Back!" *Missionhurst* (June–July 1972): 4–5.

27. J. Danièlou, *Le mystère du salut des nations* (Paris), 55; in English see *Salvation of the Nations* (Notre Dame, Ind.: University of Notre Dame Press, 1962).

28. Anselme Sanon, "Cultural Rooting of the Liturgy in Africa," 64–65.

29. Cyprian Davis, *The History of Black Catholics in the United States* (New York: Crossroad Publishing Co., 1990), 260.

30. United States Catholic Conference, *In Spirit and Truth: Black Catholic Reflections on the Order of Mass* (Washington, D.C.: NCCB/USCC, 1988), Preface, 1–2.

31. USCC/NCCB, *Plenty Good Room: The Spirit and Truth of African American Catholic Worship* (Washington, D.C.: United States Catholic Conference, 1990), especially 62–71.

32. Videotapes may be obtained from AMEN Ministries & Foundation, P.O. Box 10223, Washington, DC 20018.

33. Sister Thea Bowman: the African American nun, preacher, and evangelist, whose ministry electrified the American Catholic Church before she died of cancer a few years ago.

34. See Cyprian Davis, "African American Spirituality," in Michael Downey, ed., *The New Dictionary of Catholic Spirituality* (Collegeville, Minn.: Liturgical Press, 1993), 21-24. See also Chris Nwaka Egbulem, "African Spirituality," in the same volume, 17-21.

35. The "kente" is a multicolored, hand-woven royal material from the Ashanti people of Ghana. Because of its religious, political, and economic importance, it has been adopted by many as a symbol of African culture. It is today worn and used to decorate sanctuaries in black churches all over the world.

36. As cited by Jean Evenou in *Notitiae* 24 (1988): 456.